Devon, Cornwall & the Southwest

Publisher: David Watchus
Managing Editor: Isla Love
Senior Editor: Donna Wood
Senior Designer: Kat Mead
Picture Research: Lesley Grayson
Cartographic Editor: Geoff Chapman
Cartographic Production: Anna Thompson

Produced by AA Publishing

Published by AA Publishing (a trading name of Automobile Association Developments Limited, whose registered office is Fanum House, Basing View, Basingstoke, Hampshire RG21 4EA; registered number 1878835).

A03033c

ISBN-10: 0-7495-5190-9
ISBN-13: 978-0-7495-5190-2

A CIP catalogue record for this book is available from the British Library.

The contents of this book are believed correct at the time of printing. Nevertheless, the publishers cannot be held responsible for any errors or omissions or for changes in the details given in this book or for the consequences of any reliance on the information it provides. We have tried to ensure accuracy in this book, but things do change and we would be grateful if readers could advise us of any inaccuracies they may encounter. This does not affect your statutory rights.

We have taken all reasonable steps to ensure that the cycle rides in this book are safe and achievable by people with a reasonable level of fitness. However, all outdoor activities involve a degree of risk and the publishers accept no responsibility for any injuries caused to readers whilst following these cycle rides. For advice on cycling in safety, see pages 10-11.

Some of the cycle rides may appear in other AA books and publications.

Visit AA Publishing's website www.theAA.com/travel

Colour reproduction by Keene Group, Andover
Printed in Italy by G Canale & C SPA

Cycle Rides

Devon, Cornwall & the Southwest

Contents

Locator map

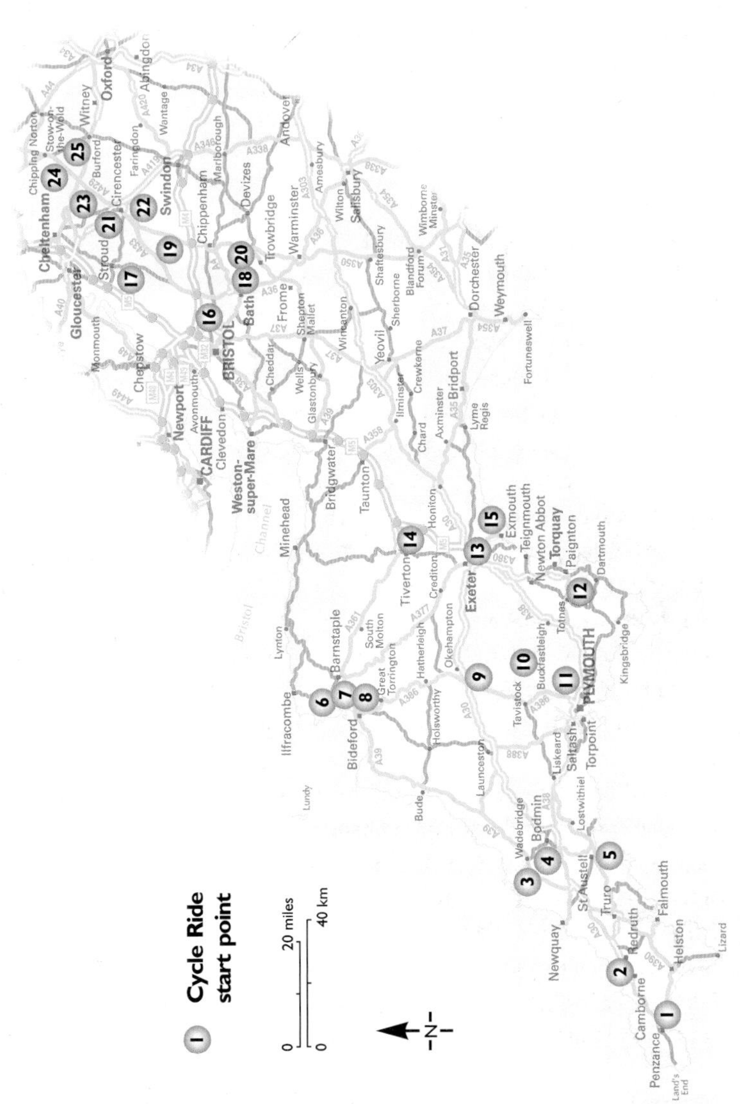

Cycle Ride start point
0
20 miles
0
40 km
N
Penzance
Land's End
Camborne
Redruth
Helston
Lizard
Falmouth
Truro
Newquay
St Austell
Wadebridge
Bodmin
Lostwithiel
Liskeard
Saltash
Torpoint
PLYMOUTH
Tavistock
Launceston
Bude
Lundy
Holsworthy
Bideford
Ilfracombe
Barnstaple
Great Torrington
Hatherleigh
Okehampton
South Molton
Lynton
Minehead
Tiverton
Crediton
Exeter
Buckfastleigh
Totnes
Kingsbridge
Dartmouth
Paignton
Torquay
Newton Abbot
Teignmouth
Exmouth
Honiton
Taunton
Bridgwater
Weston-super-Mare
Clevedon
CARDIFF
Newport
Avonmouth
Chepstow
Monmouth
BRISTOL
Cheddar
Wells
Glastonbury
Shepton Mallet
Frome
Bath
Trowbridge
Devizes
Chippenham
Swindon
Marlborough
Wantage
Abingdon
Oxford
Witney
Burford
Stow-on-the-Wold
Chipping Norton
Cheltenham
Gloucester
Stroud
Cirencester
Faringdon
Warminster
Amesbury
Andover
Wilton
Salisbury
Shaftesbury
Wincanton
Sherborne
Yeovil
Crewkerne
Ilminster
Chard
Axminster
Lyme Regis
Bridport
Dorchester
Weymouth
Fortuneswell
Blandford Forum
Wimborne Minster
Bristol Channel

Introduction to Devon, Cornwall & the Southwest

Incorporating some of Britain's most popular destinations for summer holidays and weekends away, Devon, Cornwall and the Southwest of England is ideal for cycling. This book includes a range of cycle rides, with many circular routes that follow an outward coastal path with outstanding views and then come homewards via an equally picturesque inland route. There are also lots of lovely undulating villagey routes in the Cotswolds. The coastal paths offer uninterrupted views of the sea (and often a surprising number of ups and downs), but also abundant wildlife including seabirds, wildflowers and butterflies. The cycle routes have been chosen because of the safe, traffic-free nature of the trails. The Camel Trail, the

Tarka Trail and the Plym Valley Trail are all off-road routes using trackbeds of former railway lines. Again, there's wildlife to be seen, and welcoming pubs along the way.

Many routes start from or pass through historic towns and pretty villages, such as Exeter, Barnstaple, Instow and Exmouth in Devon, and picturesque Cornish fishing villages such as Padstow. You're also never too far from a place to visit if the weather lets you down. Attractions to visit across the region vary from the magnificent house and parkland of the Saltram Estate (National Trust) in the Plym Valley and Gloucestershire's Cotswold Water Park, to Chedworth Roman Villa and the splendid stone aqueducts and magnificent scenery of the Kennet and Avon Canal. Keen gardeners are spoilt for choice in Cornwall. The ride from Pentewan has an optional loop to the Lost Gardens of Heligan, and you'll need a full day to see everything that the Eden Project has to offer.

If you prefer a historical element to your ride, take in Bath's Roman spa and 18th-century architecture, Malmesbury's Benedictine abbey ruins, or admire St Michael's Mount from the Marazion ride.

Below: The River Fowey in Cornwall

Using this book

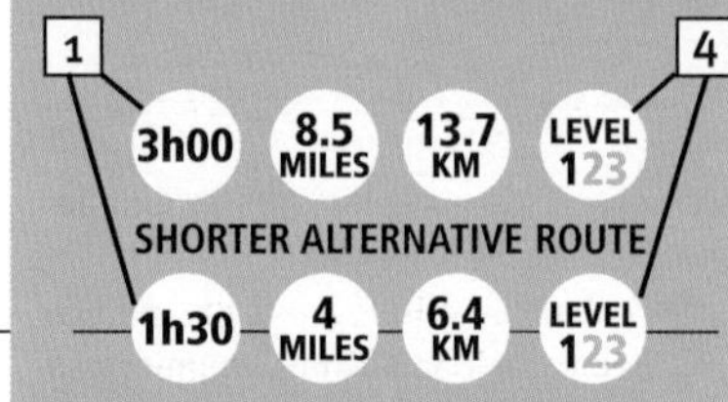

2 **MAP:** OS Explorer OL24 White Peak

3 **START/FINISH:** Rudyard Old Station, grid ref SJ955579

TRAILS/TRACKS: old railway trackbed

LANDSCAPE: wooded lake shore, peaceful pastures and meadows

PUBLIC TOILETS: Rudyard village

5 **TOURIST INFORMATION:** Leek, tel 01538 483741

6 **CYCLE HIRE:** none near by

THE PUB: The Abbey Inn, Leek, see 'Directions', page 9

7 ❗ Take care along the banks of the lake – keep well away from the shore line

Each cycle ride has a panel giving essential information for the cyclist, including the distance, terrain, nature of the paths, nearest public toilets and cycle hire.

1 **MINIMUM TIME:** The time stated for completing each ride is the estimated minimum time that a reasonably fit family group of cyclists would take to complete the circuit. This does not allow for rest or refreshment stops.

2 **MAPS:** Each route is shown on a detailed map. However, some detail is lost because of the restrictions imposed by scale, so for this reason, we recommend that you use the maps in conjunction with a more detailed Ordnance Survey map. The relevant Ordnance Survey Explorer map appropriate for each cycle ride is listed.

3 **START/FINISH:** Here we indicate the start location and parking area. There is a six-figure grid reference prefixed by two letters showing which 100km square of the National Grid it refers to. You'll find more information on grid references on most Ordnance Survey maps.

4 **LEVEL OF DIFFICULTY:** The cycle rides have been graded simply (1 to 3) to give an indication of their relative difficulty. Easier routes, such as those with little total ascent, on easy paths or level trails, or those covering shorter distances, are graded 1. The hardest routes, either because they include a lot of ascent, greater distances, or are across hilly, more demanding terrains, are graded 3.

5 **TOURIST INFORMATION:** The nearest tourist information office and contact number is given for further local information, in particular opening details for the attractions listed in the 'Where to go from here' section.

6 **CYCLE HIRE:** We list, within reason, the nearest cycle hire shop/centre.

7 ❗ Here we highlight any potential difficulties or dangers along the route. At a glance you will know if the route is steep or crosses difficult terrain, or if a cycle ride is hilly, encounters a main road, or whether a mountain bike is essential for the off-road trails. If a particular route is only considered suitable for older, fitter children we say so in this section.

About the pubs

Generally, all the pubs featured are on the cycle route. Some are close to the start/finish point, others are at the midway point, and occasionally, the recommended pub is a short drive from the start/finish point. We have included a cross-section of pubs, from homely village locals and isolated rural gems to traditional inns and upmarket country pubs which specialise in food. What they all have in common is that they serve food and welcome children.

The description of the pub is intended to convey its history and character and in the 'food' section we list a selection of dishes which indicate the style of food available. Under 'family facilities', we say if the pub offers a children's menu or smaller portions of adult dishes, and whether the pub has a family room, high chairs, baby-changing facilities, or toys. There is detail on the garden, terrace, and any play area.

DIRECTIONS: If the pub is very close to the start point we say 'see Getting to the Start'. If the pub is on the route the relevant direction/map location number is given, in addition to general directions. In some cases the pub is a short drive away from the finish point, so we give detailed directions to the pub from the end of the route.

PARKING: The number of parking spaces is given. All but a few of the rides start away from the pub. If the pub car park is the parking/start point, then we have been given permission by the landlord to print the fact. You should always let the landlord or a member of staff know that you are using the car park before setting off.

OPEN: If the pub is open all week we state 'daily' and if it's open throughout the day we say 'all day', otherwise we just give the days/sessions the pub is closed.

FOOD: If the pub serves food all week we state 'daily' and if food is served throughout the day we say 'all day', otherwise we just give days/sessions when food is not served.

BREWERY/COMPANY: This is the name of the brewery to which the pub is tied or the pub company that owns it. 'Free house' means that the pub is independently owned and run.

REAL ALE: We list the regular real ales available on handpump. 'Guest beers' indicates that the pub rotates beers from a number of microbreweries.

ROOMS: We list the number of bedrooms and how many are en suite. For prices please call the pub.

Please note that pubs change hands frequently and new chefs are employed, so menu details and facilities may change at short notice. Not all the pubs featured in this guide are listed in the *AA Pub Guide*. For information on those that are, including AA-rated accommodation, and for a comprehensive selection of pubs across Britain, please refer to the *AA Pub Guide* or see the AA's website www.theAA.com

Alternative refreshment stops

At a glance you will see if there are other pubs or cafés along the route. If there are no other places on the route, we list the nearest village or town where you can find somewhere else to eat and drink.

☛ Where to go from here

Many of the routes are short and may only take a few hours. You may wish to explore the surrounding area after lunch or before tackling the route, so we have selected a few attractions with children in mind.

Cycling in safety

CYCLING

Cycling is a fun activity which children love, and teaching your child to ride a bike and going on family cycling trips are rewarding experiences. Not only is cycling a great way to travel, but as a regular form of exercise it can make an invaluable contribution to a child's health and fitness, and increase their confidence and sense of independence.

However, the growth of motor traffic has made Britain's roads increasingly dangerous and unattractive to cyclists. Cycling with children is an added responsibility and, as with everything, there is a risk when taking them out for a day's cycling. In recent years many measures have been taken to address this, including the on-going development of the National Cycle Network (8,000 miles utilising quiet lanes and traffic-free paths) and local designated off-road routes for families, such as converted railway lines, canal towpaths and forest tracks.

In devising the cycle rides in this guide, every effort has been made to use these designated cycle paths, or to link them with quiet country lanes and waymarked byways and bridleways. Unavoidably, in a few cases, some relatively busy B-roads have been used to link the quieter, more attractive routes.

Rules of the road

- Ride in single file on narrow and busy roads.
- Be alert, look and listen for traffic, especially on narrow lanes and blind bends and be extra careful when descending steep hills, as loose gravel can lead to an accident.
- In wet weather make sure you keep a good distance between you and other riders.
- Make sure you indicate your intentions clearly.
- Brush up on *The Highway Code* before venturing out on to the road.

Off-road safety code of conduct

- Only ride where you know it is legal to do so. It is forbidden to cycle on public footpaths, marked in yellow. The only 'rights of way' open to cyclists are bridleways (blue markers) and unsurfaced tracks, known as byways, which are open to all traffic and waymarked in red.
- Canal towpaths: you need a permit to cycle on some stretches of towpath (www.waterscape.com). Remember that access paths can be steep and slippery and always get off and push your bike under low bridges and by locks.
- Always yield to walkers and horses, giving adequate warning of your approach.
- Don't expect to cycle at high speeds.
- Keep to the main trail to avoid any unnecessary erosion to the area beside the trail and to prevent skidding, especially if it is wet.
- Remember the Country Code.

Cycling with children

Children can use a child seat from the age of eight months, or from the time they can hold themselves upright. There are a number of child seats available which fit on the front or rear of a bike and towable two-seat trailers are worth investigating. 'Trailer bicycles', suitable for five- to ten-year-olds, can be attached to the rear of an adult's bike, so that the adult has control, allowing the child to pedal if he/she wishes. Family cycling can be made easier by using a tandem, as it can carry a child seat and tow trailers. 'Kiddy-cranks' for shorter legs can be fitted to the rear seat tube, enabling either parent to take their child out cycling. With older children it is better to purchase the right size bike rather than one that is too big, as an oversized bike will be difficult to control, and potentially dangerous.

Preparing your bicycle

A basic routine includes checking the wheels for broken spokes or excess play in the bearings, and checking the tyres for punctures, undue wear and the correct tyre pressures. Ensure that the brake blocks are firmly in place and not worn, and that cables are not frayed or too slack. Lubricate hubs, pedals, gear mechanisms and cables. Make sure you have a pump, a bell, a rear rack to carry panniers and, if cycling at night, a set of working lights.

Preparing yourself

Equipping the family with cycling clothing need not be an expensive exercise. Comfort is the key when considering what to wear. Essential items for well-being on a bike are padded cycling shorts, warm stretch leggings (avoid tight-fitting and seamed trousers like jeans or baggy tracksuit trousers that may become caught in the chain), stiff-soled training shoes, and a wind and waterproof jacket. Fingerless gloves will add to your comfort.

A cycling helmet provides essential protection if you fall off your bike, so they are particularly recommended for young children learning to cycle.

Wrap your child up with several layers in colder weather. Make sure you and those with you are easily visible by car drivers and other road users, by wearing light-coloured or luminous clothing in daylight and reflective strips or sashes in failing light and when it is dark.

What to take with you

Invest in a pair of medium-sized panniers (rucksacks are unwieldy and can affect balance) to carry the necessary gear for you and your family for the day. Take extra clothes with you, the amount depending on the season, and always pack a light wind/waterproof jacket. Carry a basic tool kit (tyre levers, adjustable spanner, a small screwdriver, puncture repair kit, a set of Allen keys) and practical spares, such as an inner tube, a universal brake/gear cable, and a selection of nuts and bolts. Also, always take a pump and a strong lock.

Cycling, especially in hilly terrain and off-road, saps energy, so take enough food and drink for your outing. Always carry plenty of water, especially in hot and humid weather conditions. Consume high-energy snacks like cereal bars, cake or fruits, eating little and often to combat feeling weak and tired. Remember that children get thirsty (and hungry) much more quickly than adults so always have food and diluted juices available for them.

And finally, the most important advice of all–enjoy yourselves!

1 Marazion to Penzance

Enjoy an easy ride along one of south Cornwall's most beautiful bays.

St Michael's Mount

Marazion – and the whole of Mount's Bay – is dominated by the rocky bulk of St Michael's Mount, accessible by foot via the 600yd (549m) causeway at low tide, and by ferry from the beach when the tide is up (weather permitting). This extraordinary granite outcrop is topped by a medieval castle, dating from the 12th century and now mainly in the care of the National Trust. Originally the site of a Benedictine priory, it has been the home of the St Aubyn family for over 300 years. There is also a 14th-century church on the rock, as well as a pub, restaurant and shops round the little harbour, and a private garden with limited opening times. Marazion Marsh, passed on the right of the road near the start of the ride, is the largest reedbed in Cornwall. An RSPB nature reserve, this area of reedbeds, open water and willow carr attracts overwintering bitterns, sedge, Cetti's and reed warblers, butterflies and damselflies. There is a hide from which the birds can be watched (including the rare, spotted crake) and good access via boardwalks.

the ride

1 This ride is part of the First and Last Trail, the first stretch of the Cornish Way long-distance cycle route, which starts at Land's End and runs for 180 miles (288km) through the county. Marazion, where this ride starts, is Cornwall's oldest charter town, dating from 1257. Its unusual name comes from the Cornish 'marghas yow' – Thursday market. Marazion was the main trading port in Mount's Bay until Penzance overtook it in the 16th century. It's worth having a look around this attractive village before you set off.

From the car park cycle uphill (away from the beach) onto West End. (The Godolphin Arms can be found by turning right.) Turn left along **West End** and cycle out of the village. There is a parking area on the left along much of this road, so look out for people opening their car doors suddenly. **Marazion Marsh** lies to the right.

2 Where the road bears right to cross the Penzance to Exeter main railway line, keep straight ahead through a **parking area**, with the Pizza Shack (and toilets behind) on the right. Again, take care cycling through the car park.

The medieval castle atop St Michael's Mount, seen from across the river

1

1h30 | 5 MILES | 8 KM | LEVEL 123

MAP: OS Explorer 102 Land's End
START/FINISH: The car park adjacent to The Godolphin Arms, Marazion, grid ref: SW516306
TRAILS/TRACKS: short stretch of road, track generally level, rough and bumpy in places
LANDSCAPE: village, beach, seaside, townscape
PUBLIC TOILETS: on Points **2** and **3** of the route, and in the car park at Penzance
TOURIST INFORMATION: Penzance, tel 01736 362207
CYCLE HIRE: The Cycle Centre, Penzance, tel 01736 351671
THE PUB: The Godolphin Arms, Marazion
! Short stretch of road at start and finish, one car park to be negotiated

Getting to the start

From Penzance, take the A30 past the heliport. At the second roundabout turn right, signed Marazion. The Godolphin Arms car park is signed right (towards the beach).

Why do this cycle ride?

This level, easy, there-and-back route along the edge of Mount's Bay, with spectacular views over St Michael's Mount, is an ideal option for families with young children. With just a short road stretch at the start and finish, the ride runs along the back of the huge expanse of sands between Marazion and Penzance, originally a tiny fishing community, today popular with tourists.

Researched and written by: Sue Viccars

3 Keep cycling ahead and leave the car park to the left of the old station building (now converted into the **Station pub**), to join a level track that runs along the back of the beach. Follow this easy track, passing another block of public toilets on your right.

St Michael's Mount, seen from Marazion

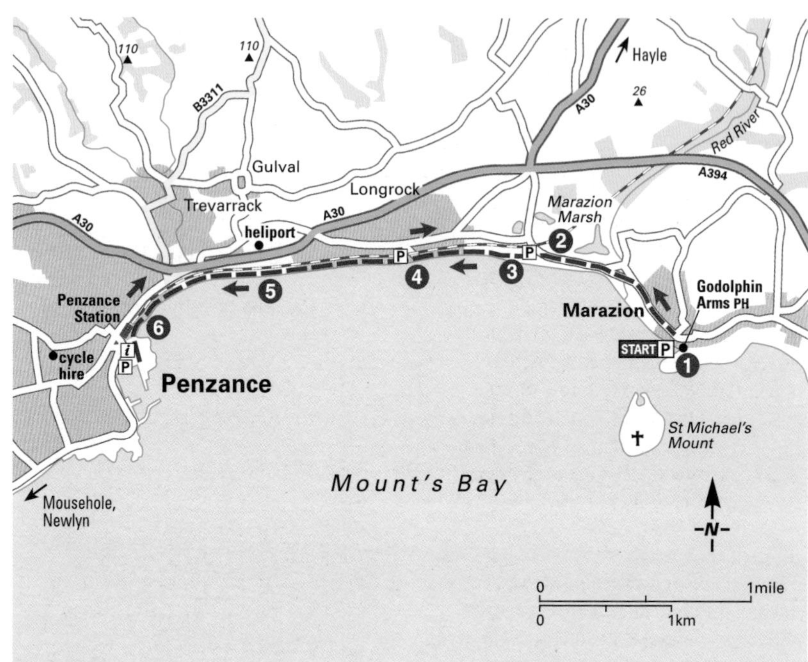

4 Take care where the track drops to meet an entrance road to a **beachside car park** (there are warning notices 'Give way to traffic'). Pass through the parking area and continue along the track, with the railway close by on the right.

5 Pass the **heliport**, from which helicopters fly regularly to the Isles of Scilly, which lie more than 17 miles (28 km) southwest of Land's End (day trips are available). Good views open up ahead towards Penzance.

6 On approaching the station the track narrows into a concrete walkway and becomes much busier, so look out for pedestrians. Follow the track into the car park by Penzance railway and bus station, with the **tourist information centre** to the right. This is where you should turn round and return to Marazion. The First and Last Trail actually runs along the road to Newlyn and beyond, but is pretty busy in terms of traffic and is not recommended for families with young children.

There is a lot to see in Penzance, however, which developed as in important pilchard fishing centre in medieval times. Penzance, Newlyn and Mousehole (along the coast to the west) were all destroyed by Spanish raiders in 1595, but by the early 17th century Penzance's fortunes had revived on account of the export of tin from local mines, and it became a fashionable place to live. The coming of the Great Western Railway in Victorian times gave the town another boost and it is now the main centre in Penwith (the far western part of Cornwall). The harbour is always full of interest, and it is from here that the RMV *Scillonian* makes regular sailings to the Isles of Scilly.

The Godolphin Arms

Located right at the water's edge opposite St Michael's Mount, The Godolphin Arms affords superb views across the bay. It's so close that the sea splashes at the windows in the winter and you can watch the movement of seals, dolphins, ferries and fishing boats. From the traditional wood-floored bar and beer terrace to the light and airy restaurant and most of the bedrooms, the Mount is clearly visible.

Food

The bar menu offers light meals and snacks, all made with fresh produce, of which the proprietors are justly proud. Club sandwiches and freshly buttered cod are current favourites, but the menu changes constantly, with the onus on seafood.

Family facilities

There's an area set aside for families, and high chairs and baby-changing facilities for young children. Smaller portions from the main menu and a children's menu featuring all the old favourites are available. There are two family bedrooms. The beach is just below the pub's rear terrace.

about the pub

The Godolphin Arms
West End, Marazion
Penzance, Cornwall TR17 0EN
Tel 01736 710202
www.godolphinarms.co.uk

DIRECTIONS: see Getting to the start
PARKING: 70, next to pub; pay and display
OPEN: daily; all day
FOOD: daily; all day in summer
BREWERY/COMPANY: free house
REAL ALE: Sharp's Special and Doom Bar, Skinner's Spriggan
ROOMS: 10 en suite

Alternative refreshment stops

There are plenty of pubs, cafés and restaurants in Marazion and Penzance.

☛ Where to go from here

Head for Newlyn where you will find Britain's only working salt pilchard factory, the Pilchard Works, where you can experience at first hand a Cornish factory that has continued producing salt pilchards for over 90 years (www.pilchardworks.co.uk). Art lovers should visit the Penlee House Gallery and Museum in Penzance (www.penleehouse.org.uk) to learn more about the Newlyn School of Artists and view one of the regular exhibitions. Kids will enjoy a visit to the Lighthouse Centre in Penzance or to the Wild Bird Hospital and Sanctuary in Mousehole. For information about St Michael's Mount see www.nationaltrust.org.uk

2

On the Portreath tramroad

A fascinating exploration of Cornwall's industrial past.

Mining memorabilia

This ride is just bursting with industrial and natural history. The Portreath tramroad (along which wagons were originally drawn by horses) was the first of its kind in Cornwall, and the section to Scorrier was active from 1812 until the mid 1860s, linking important tin- and copper-mining areas with the harbour at Portreath. The Wheal Busy Loop, positively stuffed with old engine houses, gives an indication of how much industrial activity went on in this now somewhat bleak area in the 18th and 19th centuries. One of the first Newcomen steam engines was built here in 1725, and later Wheal Busy boasted the first James Watt steam engine in Cornwall. Nearby Chacewater was once a prosperous mining village, as evidenced by the number of fine Georgian and Victorian shop fronts preserved today.

Unity Wood is full of old shafts and workings too, and mining for tin here dates from opencast methods (known as 'coffinworks') in medieval times. Today these tranquil remains provide suitable conditions for a good range of flora and fauna: the common blue and green hairstreak butterfly, pipistrelles and greater horseshoe bats (roosting in the deserted mine shafts), and dragonflies and damselflies dancing above the old mine ponds.

the ride

1 From the car park turn left and follow it inland past the **Portreath Arms Hotel** (left). Just past the hotel bear left along narrow Sunny Vale Road. Where this bears right to rejoin the B3300 bear left onto the **tramway**. Follow this through woodland and over the access road to a reservoir. Continue through woodland, then fields, eventually reaching a drive with a white cottage on the left. Keep ahead along a narrow lane to reach a minor road. Drop down to cross the road at **Cambrose**.

2 Turn left and cycle along the pavement (cycle lane), following the road past **Elm Farm** (left). Around 500yds (457m) later, where the road bears left, turn right on a quiet lane to a T-junction at **Lower Forge**. Cross the road and keep ahead along a lane. Keep ahead at the next T-junction onto the tramway again. Follow this to its end at North Downs (1.75 miles/2.8km); turn left to meet a road. Turn right along the pavement (cycle lane) to the roundabout.

(For the Fox and Hounds pub – and so **the shorter route** – keep ahead round the right edge of the roundabout to cross the A30. Follow the pavement round to the right and cross the road by the Crossroads Motel. Follow the road under the railway bridge and bear left; the pub will be found on the right.)

3 For the **Wheal Busy Loop** – which is quite hard, but highly recommended – turn left across the road and follow the pavement, keeping the roundabout right. Keep uphill past another small roundabout, then Smokey Joe's café on the left. At the top of the hill turn right to cross the **A30**.

4 Just over the bridge turn left down a rough track. Bear left at **Boscawen Farm** and follow the track as it undulates past the remains of Boscawen Mine. Pass **Wheal Busy chapel** left, to reach a lane junction. Keep ahead; 109 yards (100m) on turn right down a rough bridleway. Turn right on a track at the bottom. Drop gently downhill, passing to the left of **old mine buildings** at Wheal Busy. Keep ahead and cross a small lane, then head steadily uphill, bearing left at the top to meet a road.

5 Cross over and follow a track through a small parking area and downhill past Killifreth Mine's **Hawke's Shaft pumping house** (with the tallest chimney stack in Cornwall, and shafts up to 600ft/183m deep). Enter **Unity Woods**; keep left at the fork and follow the bumpy track downhill to a junction.

6 Turn right, rejoining the **tramway**. Follow the track out of the woods, with fields right and a road (B3298) left. Cross the road where signed – take care – and continue along the track to the left of the road. At the junction turn left to push along the pavement. After 109 yards (100m) turn right to cross the road, passing to the right of the Fox and Hounds pub. At the next road turn left and pass under the railway bridge. At the T-junction by the **Crossroads Motel**, cross over and turn right on the pavement to cross the A30 and rejoin the outward route.

The Portreath tramroad

3h00 – 13.5 MILES – 21.7 KM – LEVEL 123

SHORTER ALTERNATIVE ROUTE

2h00 – 10 MILES – 16 KM – LEVEL 123

MAP: OS Explorer 104 Redruth & St Agnes

START/FINISH: beach car park in Portreath, grid ref: SW654453

TRAILS/TRACKS: mainly well-surfaced track, extension rough and rocky, some roadwork

LANDSCAPE: woodland and fields, heath, old mine workings

PUBLIC TOILETS: none on route

TOURIST INFORMATION: Helston, tel 01326 565431

CYCLE HIRE: Elm Farm, on the tramroad near Portreath, tel 01209 891498

THE PUB: Basset Arms, Portreath

! Busy roads with good, marked pavements and some rough sections on the Wheal Busy Loop

Getting to the start

Portreath is about 4 miles (6.4km) north west of Redruth, and is signed off the A30 on the B3300. Park in the car park by the beach.

Why do this cycle ride?

The Coast-to-Coast Trail follows the Portreath tramroad as far as Scorrier. This ride takes you into the heart of old industrial Cornwall, following a trail that runs across the county for 11 miles (17.5km) to Devoran on Restronguet Creek. The optional Wheal Busy Loop explores an area peppered with old engine houses.

Researched and written by: Sue Viccars

2

Portreath CORNWALL

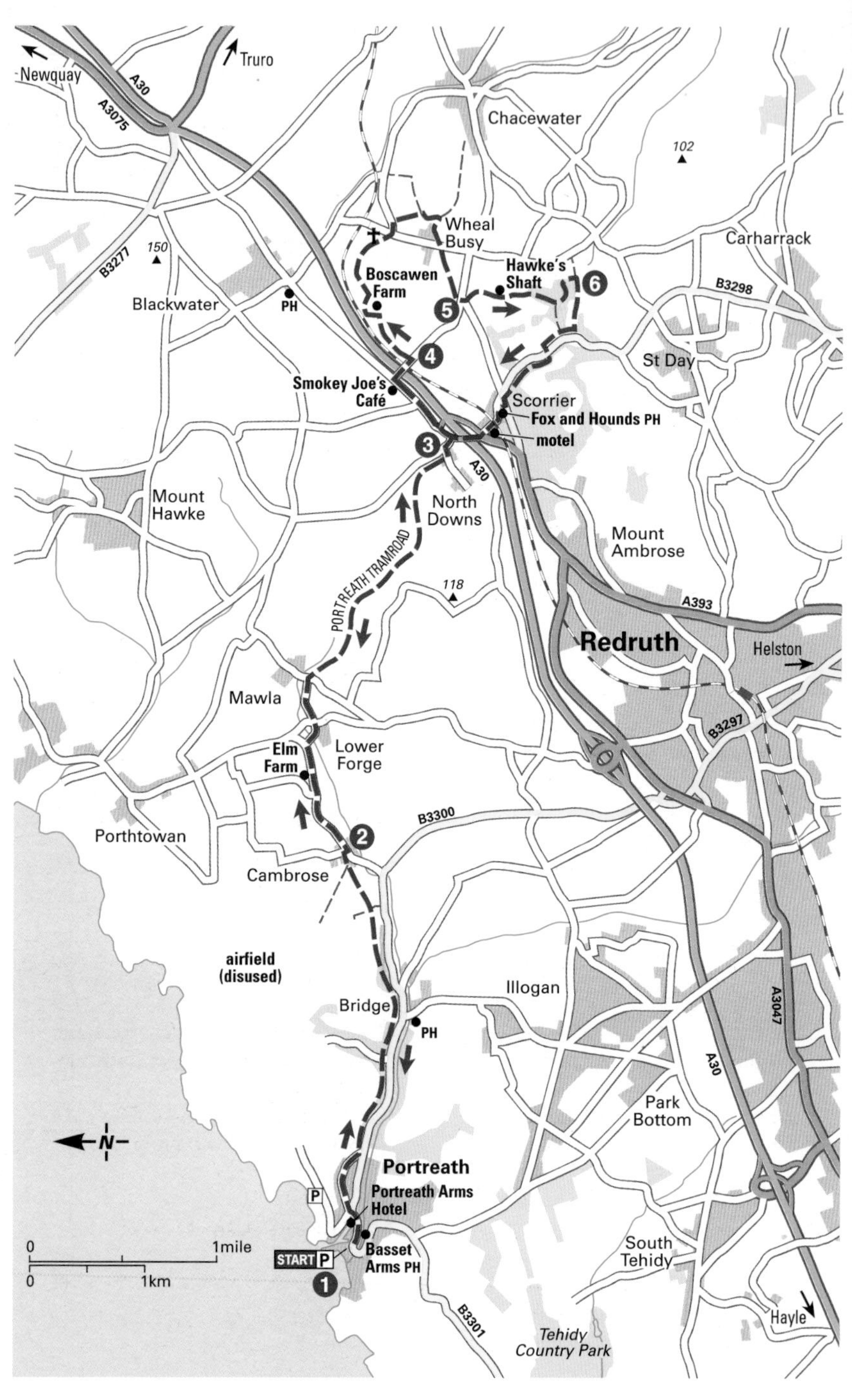

Basset Arms

2

The Basset Arms is a typical Cornish cottage, built as a pub in the early 19th century to serve the harbour workers, with plenty of tin mining and shipwreck memorabilia adorning the low-beamed interior. Today, it serves the many cyclists using the mineral tramways cycle path to Devoran – the pub is conveniently located at the start point – and the beach is just a short stroll away. There are cycle racks in the car park and a sunny terrace and garden for summer days. In winter, there's a comfortable bar with an open fire and a big conservatory dining room to relax in after the ride.

Food

Bar food is hearty and traditional, ranging from bacon sandwiches, filled jacket potatoes and seaside salads (prawn or Cornish yarg), to grills with all the trimmings and daily specials like steak and ale pie and fresh local fish. There are good value Sunday roast lunches and summer weekend barbecues held in the garden.

Family facilities

Children are welcome throughout the pub and youngsters have a standard children's menu to choose from. There is also an adventure play area in the garden.

Alternative refreshment stops

There's at least one beach café and the Portreath Arms Hotel in Portreath, while on the route you'll find the Fox and Hounds pub on the shorter loop.

☛ Where to go from here

At Pool near Redruth you can see impressive relics of the tin-mining industry at the Cornish Mines and Engines, namely great beam engines and a fascinating industrial heritage centre in a converted mine. Informative guided tours take you through the ancient process of cider making at the Cornish Cyder Farm at Penhallow (www.thecornishcyderfarm.co.uk). Head for Truro and spend some time at the Royal Cornwall Museum and learn more about the county in well laid-out galleries displaying artefacts from the stone age, Cornish wildlife and 21st-century studio pottery (www.royalcornwallmuseum.org.uk).

about the pub

Basset Arms
Tregea Terrace, Portreath
Redruth, Cornwall TR16 4NG
Tel 01209 842077
www.ccinns.co.uk

DIRECTIONS: from the beach car park turn right and follow the road round to the left to the pub

PARKING: 25

OPEN: daily; all day Saturday and Sunday and July to September

FOOD: daily

BREWERY/COMPANY: Coast and Country Inns

REAL ALE: Sharp's Doom Bar, Wadworth 6X, changing guest ale

The Camel Trail – Edmonton to Padstow

Fabulous views and wonderful birdlife make this section of the Camel Trail a delight at any time of year.

Padstow and Prideaux Place

Although Padstow is frequently almost overrun with visitors – especially so since chef Rick Stein took up residence – it is still an attractive little town with an interesting maritime history. St Petroc is said to have come here from Wales in the 6th century AD and founded a monastery which was later sacked by the Vikings in the 10th century. The name Padstow comes from 'Petroc stow' (Petroc's church). Being the only decent harbour on the north coast between Bude and St Ives, Padstow was once the fourth most important port in the country, exporting copper and tin, slate and farm produce. Padstow's famous ancient and pagan Obby Oss ceremony takes place every year on May Day. Rumour has it that it even deterred a party of raiding Frenchmen during the Hundred Years' War!

The Prideaux family – whose origins date back to the 11th century – built their home, Prideaux Place, above the town in the 16th century, and their descendants still live there. This beautiful Elizabethan mansion – now open to the public – is

Right: Padstow Harbour

2h00 | 10 MILES | 16.1 KM | LEVEL 123

surrounded by gardens laid out in Georgian and Victorian times. A tunnel, giving the family private access, leads from the grounds to St Petroc's Church.

the ride

1 The Quarryman Inn is a fascinating place. Behind the pub are two terraces of stone cottages, originally homes for workers at the quarries (Point 3); when these fell into disuse in the early 20th century the building became a TB isolation hospital. Today it is a very welcoming pub. From the **car park** turn right. At the crossroads turn left and enjoy a lovely downhill run, with increasingly good views over the River Camel and rolling farmland beyond. The Camel was known as the Allen river until 1870, thought to derive from the Irish word *alain*, for beautiful: it's easy to see why. Pass through the hamlet at **Tregunna** and follow the lane over a bridge to its end. Turn right down a narrow earthy path to reach the trail.

2 Turn right and follow the trail along the edge of the **estuary**. At low tide it's almost like cycling along the edge of a beach as the river is flanked by broad expanses of sand and the views are superb. The creeks and sandbanks attract wintering wildfowl – widgeon, goldeneye, long tailed duck – as well as many divers and waders, spring and autumn migrants. Look out for curlew, oystercatcher, shelduck and little egret. One of the main reasons for constructing the railway was to transport sea sand, rich in lime, from the estuary, to fertilise farmland away from the coast. Granite, slate, tin, iron and copper from mines on Bodmin Moor were exported.

MAP: OS Explorer 106 Newquay & Padstow

START/FINISH: The Quarryman Inn, Edmonton; grid ref: SW964727

TRAILS/TRACKS: well-surfaced former railway track

LANDSCAPE: river estuary, rolling farmland

PUBLIC TOILETS: Padstow

TOURIST INFORMATION: Padstow, tel 01841 533449

CYCLE HIRE: Camel Trail Cycle Hire, Wadebridge, tel 01208 814104

THE PUB: The Quarryman Inn, Edmonton

! Padstow is very busy at holiday times – leave your bikes at the secure lock-up on the quay and go into town on foot

Getting to the start

Edmonton is west of Wadebridge. Bypass Wadebridge on the A39 signed 'St Columb Major/Padstow'. About 1 mile (1.6km) after crossing the Camel turn right, before Whitecross, on a lane signed 'Edmonton'.

Why do this cycle ride?

If you prefer to avoid Wadebridge, try this route to access the lower part of the Camel Trail. It is busier than the Dunmere to Wadebridge stretch, but the views make it worthwhile, and starting from the Quarryman's Arms is a bonus. If you want to keep away from crowds of people, turn round on the edge of Padstow, or just dive in quickly for an ice cream. If you like birdlife don't forget your binoculars.

Researched and written by: Sue Viccars

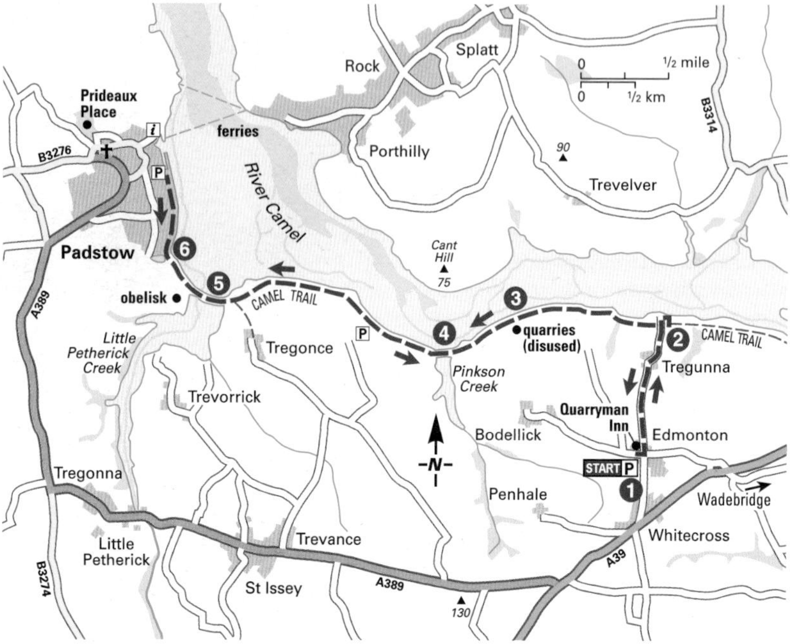

3 A long cutting ends at the spoil heaps of the old slate quarries, with rounded, wooded **Cant Hill** opposite. The estuary is widening as it approaches the sea; there's a glimpse of **Padstow** ahead on the left bank. The mouth of the Camel Estuary is marred by the notorious Doom Bar, a shifting sandbank responsible for more than 300 shipwrecks from 1760 to 1920. If you're cycling the Camel Trail on a sunny day it's hard to imagine such disasters.

4 Continue past **Pinkson Creek** – you may see herons – and continue on to pass the parking area at **Oldtown Cove**. Once through the next cutting you'll get fantastic views towards Rock, on the other side of the estuary, with Brea Hill and Daymer Bay beyond, and out to the open sea. The trail bears away from the estuary through a cutting.

5 Cross the bridge over **Little Petherick Creek**. The Saints' Way, a 30-mile (48km) walking route, links Fowey on the south coast with Padstow's St Petroc's Church. It runs along the edge of the creek and past the **obelisk** (commemorating Queen Victoria's jubilee in 1887) on Dennis Hill, seen ahead. The creek is also an important habitat for little egret and a good range of wading birds.

6 Follow the trail past a lake on the left and then past houses on the edge of Padstow, with moored boats on the water right. **Rock**, opposite, is a popular sailing and watersports venue, and there's always masses to watch on the water. The trail ends at the **quay** and car park; dismount at this point to explore the town, which has some interesting little shops. Retrace your tracks along the Camel Trail to Edmonton.

The Quarryman Inn

You can expect a genuine warm welcome at this 18th-century village inn that evolved around a carefully reconstructed slate-built courtyard of old quarrymen's cottages. Gas heaters warm this area on cooler days and it is a lovely sheltered spot to enjoy a drink or evening meal. Among the features at this unusual pub are several bow windows, one is a delightful stained-glass quarryman panel, and interesting old brass optics above the fireplace in the beamed bar. Tip-top ale comes from local small breweries and the menu includes fresh local fish.

Food

At lunch tuck into roast ham sandwiches or filled Italian bread (smoked bacon, Brie and cranberry), Cornish fish pie or the curry of the day. Evening additions include tempura prawns with sweet chilli sauce, oven-roasted lamb shank, roast duck with cherry sauce and local fish such as whole bass stuffed with bacon.

about the pub

The Quarryman Inn
Edmonton, Wadebridge
Cornwall PL27 7JA
Tel 01208 816444

DIRECTIONS: see Getting to the start
PARKING: 100
OPEN: daily; all day
FOOD: daily
BREWERY/COMPANY: free house
REAL ALE: Skinner's & Sharp's beers, Timothy Taylor Landlord, guest beers

Family facilities

Children of all ages are welcome in the pub. Smaller portions of adult meals are available for youngsters.

Alternative refreshment stops

You'll be spoilt for choice in Padstow as there are some good pubs and cafés and a few excellent restaurants.

☛ Where to go from here

Visit the Delabole Slate Quarry near Camelford, the oldest and largest working slate quarry in England. There are tours every weekday (www.delaboleslate.com). Camelford is also the location for the nation's foremost museum of cycling history, from 1818 to the present day, with over 400 cycles, cycling medals and displays of gas lighting. Overlooking the wild Cornish coast are the 13th-century ruins of Tintagel Castle, the legendary birthplace of King Arthur and home to Merlin the magician (www.english-heritage.org.uk). Close to Padstow is the Crealy Adventure Park where kids can scare themselves on the Haunted Castle ride, the Raging River Watercoaster and the Thunder Falls (www.crealy.co.uk).

4

The Camel Trail – Dunmere to Wadebridge

Enjoy a quiet and easy section of the Camel Trail along the lovely wooded banks of the River Camel.

Bodmin Moor

The River Camel rises on Bodmin Moor. Like Dartmoor, over the county boundary in Devon, it is a raised granite plateau, part of the same huge belt of ancient rock that outcrops to form Penwith in west Cornwall and the Isles of Scilly off Land's End.

Bodmin and Dartmoor are characterised by the presence of tors, heavily weathered outcrops of granite: Bodmin's most famous is the Cheesewring. The highest point on the moors is Brown Willy (1,368ft/417m) and many of Cornwall's beautiful rivers rise on the boggy moorland heights. An old name for this upland tract was 'Fowey Moor' – the source of the River Fowey lies just below Brown Willy. There is evidence of extensive Bronze Age occupation, in the unmistakable form of megalithic chambered tombs, standing stones and stone circles dating back over 4,000 years. Tin and copper were mined on the moor from the mid 18th century, and china clay – once one of Cornwall's most important sources of wealth – was mined from 1862 until 2001. Bodmin Moor is also recorded for posterity in Daphne du Maurier's classic novel *Jamaica Inn*.

the ride

1 The Camel Trail is clearly accessed from the car park. Push your bike down the steep ramp to join the **old railway track**. A granite block displays a map of the 17-mile (27.4km) trail from Poley's Bridge to Padstow. The railway line from Wadebridge to Dunmere Junction, and then to Bodmin is the third in the country, and the first steam-hauled railway in Cornwall (others used horse power). The Wadebridge to Padstow line opened in 1889 and closed in 1967. Turn left, soon crossing the **River Camel**, which reaches the sea at Padstow.

2 Continue on past the end of the Bodmin and Wenford Steam Railway at **Boscarne Junction**. Boscarne Junction was linked to the main line at Bodmin Road (now Parkway) in 1888. Pass round a staggered barrier and over a small lane; continue through **woodland**.

3 Cross the next lane via a gate (a left turn here will take you to **Nanstallon**, site of a Roman fort); you'll see the Camel Trail Tea Garden on the right. Cycle past access to the **Camel Valley Vineyard** (right) and continue through pretty, mixed woodland – oak, ash, beech, spindle, hazel and holly – with glimpses of the River Camel through the trees, left. Pass **Grogley Halt**, with picnic tables and access to the river (popular with salmon fishermen here) on the left.

Below: Taking a break on The Camel Trail

4

2h00 **10 MILES** **16.1 KM** **LEVEL 123**

MAP: OS Explorer 109 Bodmin Moor and 106 Newquay & Padstow

START/FINISH: Camel Trail car park at Dunmere, grid ref: SX047675

TRAILS/TRACKS: well-surfaced former railway track

LANDSCAPE: wooded river valley

PUBLIC TOILETS: The Platt, Wadebridge

TOURIST INFORMATION: Wadebridge, tel 08701 223337

CYCLE HIRE: Bodmin Cycle Hire, General Station, Bodmin, tel 01208 73555

THE PUB: The Borough Arms, Dunmere

! Busy road through centre of Wadebridge to rejoin the Camel Trail

Getting to the start

Bodmin lies just off the A30. From the centre of town follow signs for Wadebridge, along the A389 (Dunmere Road). After about 1 mile (1.6km) the road drops downhill. The Borough Arms will be seen on the left. Turn left through the car park into the official Camel Trail car park.

Why do this cycle ride?

This is an easy ride along a pretty, wooded section of the old Bodmin to Wadebridge railway line – now the Camel Trail – and you'll be in Wadebridge before you know it. You can extend the ride by passing through the town and rejoining the Camel Trail along the beautiful Camel estuary to Padstow (see The Camel Trail – Edmonton to Padstow).

Researched and written by: Sue Viccars

4 Pass through a cutting and then by beautiful stone and slate cottages at **Polbrock**. Pass under a bridge and look left for access to the riverbank (note: cycle racks on the side of the trail). Pass the grass-covered **Shooting Range Platform** on the left. Cross the Camel again: look ahead right to see the edge of Egloshayle, on the west bank of the Camel. The name means 'church on the estuary', and the church tower soon comes into view across the river meadows and reedbeds.

5 Pass under a small bridge to reach **Guineaport Road**. Follow this quiet residential road towards Wadebridge, passing the **old station** on the left (now the John Betjeman Centre – Sir John Betjeman is buried at St Enodoc Church, near Brea Hill on the Camel Estuary). Follow the road as it bears left to reach a roundabout, with the cinema opposite. Turn right down **The Platt** (once regularly flooded so boats were drawn up here in the 19th century). The bustling town of **Wadebridge**, dating back to the early 14th century and situated at the lowest crossing point of the Camel, makes a good focus for the ride. There are plenty of pubs and cafés, and it's worth taking a look at the much-altered medieval bridge across the Camel, believed by some to have been built on sacks of wool. Despite alterations, it maintains its sturdy traditional style.

6 If you want to keep going on the Camel Trail keep straight ahead at the next roundabout along **Eddystone Road** passing the tourist information (and various cafés) on the right. Granite for the rebuilding of the Eddystone lighthouse, off Plymouth, was shipped from Wadebridge Town Quay. At the next roundabout take the **third exit** (by the bike hire shops) and you'll be back on the Camel Trail again. Return along the trail to the car park and The Borough Arms at Dunmere.

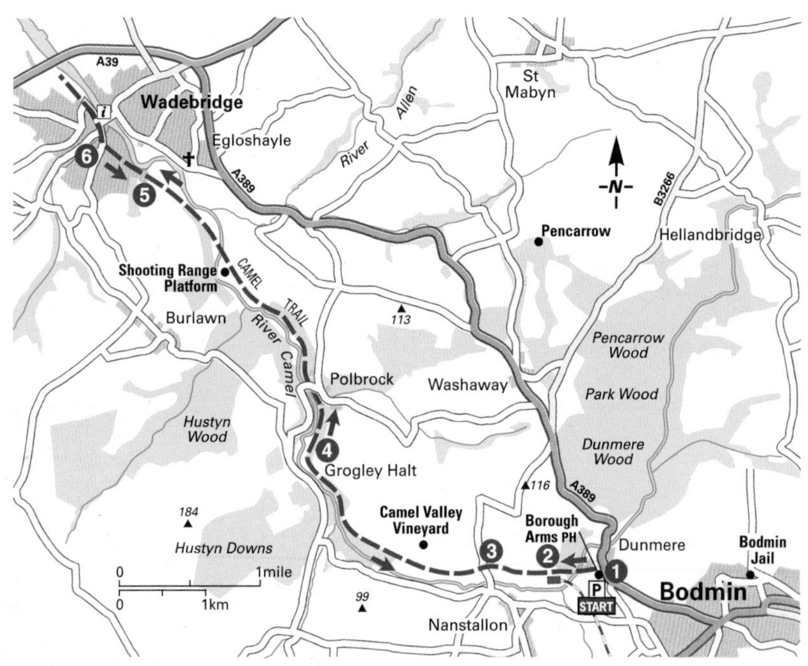

The Borough Arms

Situated in glorious countryside close to Bodmin Moor, this popular pub stands on the route of the Camel Trail and welcomes walkers and cyclists exploring this traffic-free route between Bodmin and Padstow. Much extended over recent years it makes a great spot to rest weary legs and refuel with a pint of Cornish ale and some hearty pub food. There are bike racks in the car park and children, who are really welcome, can explore the adventure playground on fine days.

about the pub

The Borough Arms
Dunmere, Bodmin
Cornwall PL31 2RD
Tel 01208 73118
www.borougharms.ukpub.net

DIRECTIONS: see Getting to the start
PARKING: 30
OPEN: daily; all day
FOOD: daily
BREWERY/COMPANY: Spirit Group
REAL ALE: Sharp's Eden Ale and Doom Bar, Skinner's beers

Food

Traditional pub fare includes a light menu of sandwiches, filled baguettes and jacket potatoes. More substantial dishes include steak and ale pie, beer battered cod and chips and lasagne, plus daily specials and a fill-your-own-plate carvery.

Family facilities

Children are allowed in the areas away from the bar and notices inform parents that children must be accompanied at all times. In addition to the family areas, there's a kid's menu, smaller portions of adult meals, high chairs and baby-changing facilities.

Alternative refreshment stops

The Camel Trail Tea Garden at Point 3 and various pubs and cafés in Wadebridge.

☛ Where to go from here

The beautifully restored steam locomotives at the Bodmin & Wenford Railway take you back to the glory days of the Great Western Railway when hordes of holidaymakers travelled this route to the sun (www.bodminandwenfordrailway.co.uk). Bodmin Gaol is a former country prison, built in 1778, with spooky underground passages where the Crown Jewels were stored during World War I. There's plenty to keep children amused at Dobwalls Family Adventure Park, with stretches of miniature American railroads to ride, and action-packed areas filled with both indoor and outdoor adventure play equipment (www.dobwallsadventurepark.co.uk).

Through the Pentewan Valley

A gentle ride along the banks of the St Austell River, with an optional extension to Heligan Gardens.

The Lost Gardens and Pentewan

Even if you don't get as far as the Lost Gardens of Heligan on your bike, you should somehow include it in your itinerary. Home of the Tremayne family for over 400 years, the story of the 'uncovering' of the gardens during the 1990s by Tim Smit (latterly of Eden Project fame) and his team is well known. But this is so much more than just a 'garden' – for a start it covers 200 acres (81ha) – there's also a subtropical jungle, farm walks, fabulous vegetable gardens, various wildlife projects, and the romantic 'Lost Valley', as well as a farm shop, an attractive restaurant, plants sales and a shop.

It's worth taking some time to have a look around Pentewan village, with its narrow streets and pleasant square. The glorious sandy beach, popular with holidaymakers, featured in the Lloyds Bank 'Black Horse' advertisements. The old harbour opposite the Ship Inn is now silted up, a recurring problem during the life of the railway due to clay waste being washed downriver from the mines. This, and the growing importance of the ports at Par and Fowey, contributed to the closure of the Pentewan railway, which never reached the Cornwall Railway's main line, in 1918.

the ride

1 From the village car park return towards the B3273 and pass through the **parking area** for Pentewan Valley Cycle Hire, and round a staggered barrier onto the trail, which initially runs levelly through marshy woodland. The trail emerges from woodland onto the banks of the **St Austell River**, with a caravan site opposite.

2 Turn right and follow the trail along the riverbank. Watch out for pedestrians as this is a popular stretch. Along part of the trail walkers have the option of taking a narrow parallel route on a bank.

Top right: The Lost Gardens of Heligan
Left: Millennium signpost

3 Note the turn-off left across the river to the Lost Gardens of Heligan. Pass round the edge of a small parking area into **King's Wood** (owned by the Woodland Trust), and follow the trail as signposted, left back onto the riverbank. Dip into woodland again, then bear right, cycling away from the river onto a **lane**, with a small parking area a little uphill to the right.

4 Turn left; passing a small parking area to meet a tarmac lane on a bend. Bear right as signed. Turn left opposite **'Brooklea'** and continue cycling on a narrow wooded path, with a caravan site left. The track bears left at **Molingey** – with the London Apprentice on the other side of the river – then right to run along the right bank of the river again. Follow this tarmac way as it bears right through fields, then left along the edge of the **water treatment works**. Turn left for 50yds (46m) to meet the B3273. Turn right along the pavement.

5 Cross the lane to **Tregorrick**, and take the **second lane** on the left (Sawles Road – unsigned). Follow this quiet country lane to its end. For St Austell (and a possible extension to the Eden Project) turn left uphill to cross the A390. For Pentewan either turn around here, or for a more pleasant alternative, turn right and cycle steeply uphill through pleasant countryside. Drop to a T-junction and turn right, steeply downhill, through Tregorrick. On meeting the B3273 turn left to return to **Pentewan**.

6 **Heligan extension**: just after passing Point 2 above, turn right to cross the river on the **footbridge** (you must dismount). On reaching the B3273, turn left.

2h30 – **10 MILES** – **16.1 KM** – **LEVEL 123**

SHORTER ALTERNATIVE ROUTE

1h30 – **7 MILES** – **11.3 KM** – **LEVEL 123**

MAP: OS Explorer 105 Falmouth & Mevagissey

START/FINISH: Pentewan Valley Cycle Hire; grid ref: SX017473

TRAILS/TRACKS: mainly well-surfaced track, some woodland paths, little roadwork

LANDSCAPE: woodland and fields, riverside, roadwork on extension

PUBLIC TOILETS: in centre of Pentewan

TOURIST INFORMATION: St Austell, tel 01726 879500

CYCLE HIRE: Pentewan Valley Cycle Hire, tel 01726 844242

THE PUB: The Ship, Pentewan

! Busy roads (in season) and steep ascent/descent on Heligan extension

Getting to the start

Pentewan lies just off the B3273, about 1.5 miles (2.4km) north of Mevagissey. Lane-side parking in Pentewan is limited, but there is a free car park. Start at the cycle hire shop.

Why do this cycle ride?

This pleasant route, which opened in 1995, follows the line of the old Pentewan railway along the tranquil St Austell river. A loop through quiet lanes provides a convenient 'turnaround', and an optional, steep extension to the Lost Gardens of Heligan for those seeking more strenuous exercise.

Researched and written by: Sue Viccars

Pass the touring park left, then turn right to cross the road as signed. Turn left with the pavement, then continue on a track. This bears right, away from the road into the Tremayne Estate woodland. Climb steadily uphill for 0.75 mile (1.2km), levelling off as the track passes beneath a road. Bear left to a fork; Mevagissey may be found via the right fork. Keep left to meet the road (note that this can be busy); turn left for 0.5 mile (0.8km) to find Heligan on the left.

7 On leaving Heligan, turn right along the road. Cycle gently downhill, with great views over St Austell Bay. Turn left on the **first narrow lane**, steeply downhill. On meeting the next minor road, turn left, even more steeply, to meet the B3273 opposite **Pentewan Sands Holiday Park**. Turn left towards the Esso garage, then right into Pentewan village.

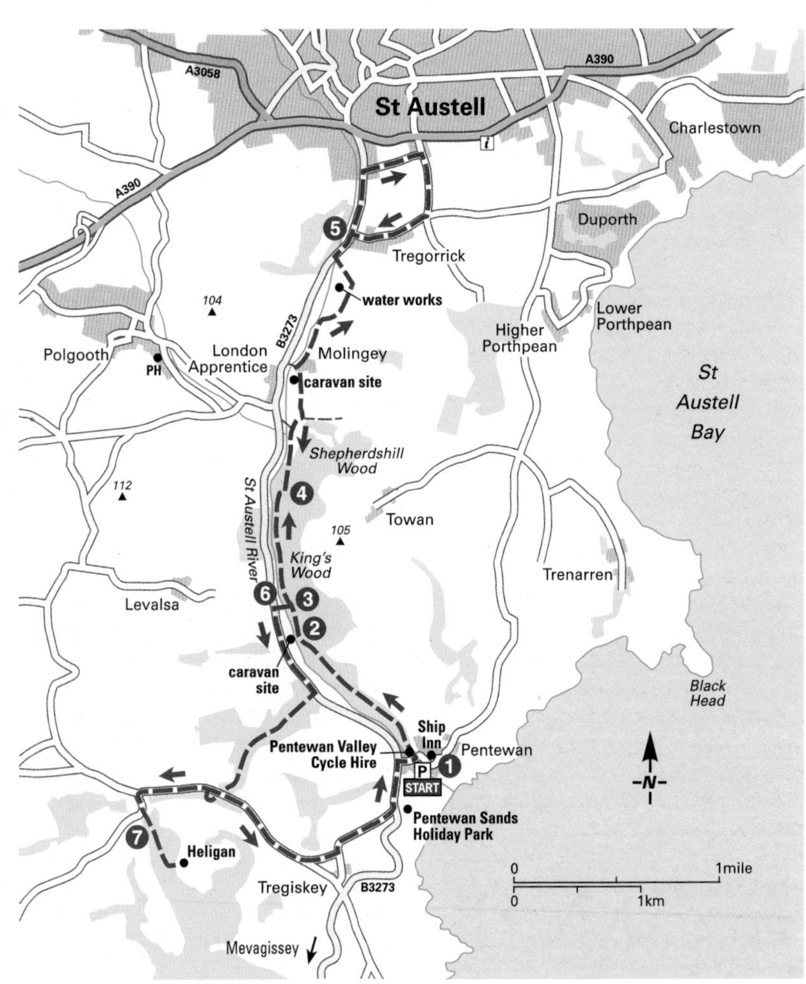

The Ship

about the pub

The Ship
West End, Pentewan
St Austell, Cornwall PL26 6BX
Tel: 01726 842855
www.staustellbrewery.co.uk

DIRECTIONS: see Getting to the start; pub on the main village street
PARKING: none
OPEN: daily; all day May to October
FOOD: daily
BREWERY/COMPANY: St Austell Brewery
REAL ALE: St Austell Tinner's Ale, Tribute and HSD

Festooned with colourful hanging baskets, the attractive Ship Inn fronts on to the main village street and is a real picture in summer, drawing in passing visitors, coast path walkers and cyclists fresh from the Pentewan Valley Trail. Tables fill early in the garden on fine days as they make the most of the pub's view across the village and the old harbour. The interior is equally appealing, with beams, shipwreck and maritime memorabilia, comfortable furnishings and a welcoming atmosphere filling the two bars, and there's the added attraction of the full complement of St Austell ales on hand-pump.

Food

Expect a traditional choice of pub meals that includes sandwiches, crusty baguettes, fisherman's lunch (smoked mackerel), steak and kidney pudding, and ham, egg and chips at lunch. Evening additions take in various grills and dishes featuring fresh local fish.

Family facilities

Children are allowed in the public bar until 9pm, and can remain unrestricted in the lounge bar, where the under 11s have a children's menu to choose from.

Alternative refreshment stops

There are cafés at the Lost Gardens of Heligan and a good choice of pubs and cafés in Pentewan.

☛ Where to go from here

For an unforgettable experience in a breathtaking location, visit the Eden Project (www.edenproject.com) north of St Austell. It is the gateway into a fascinating world of plants and human society – space age technology meets the lost world in the biggest greenhouse ever built. There are two gigantic geodesic conservatories: the Humid Tropics Biome and the Warm Temperate Biome. To view the largest display of shipwreck artefacts in Britain, head for the Charlestown Shipwreck and Heritage Centre (www.shipwreckcharlestown.com), and for more information on the Lost Gardens of Heligan visit www.heligan.com

6

The Tarka Trail – Braunton to Barnstaple

A gentle ride along the Taw estuary from historic Braunton to Barnstaple's old quayside.

Braunton Burrows

As you set off along the Tarka Trail from Braunton look right and in the distance you'll see a ridge of sand dunes (dating from the last Ice Age) – those nearest the sea are around 100ft (over 30m) high. This is Braunton Burrows, the second largest dune system in the UK, designated as an UNESCO International Biosphere Reserve in November 2002. The whole dune system is moving gradually inland, in some places as much as 10ft (3m) per year, and is well worth exploring. There are areas of managed meadowland, grassland, marsh and sandy habitats. Almost 500 different species of flowering plant have been identified, including 11 orchids. Sustainable tourism is the keyword here, and access for visitors is managed carefully so that fragile parts of the site are protected. The area is easily accessible by road or bike.

Braunton has a fascinating agricultural history, too. Between the village and the Burrows lies Braunton Great Field, a rare example of medieval strip farming. This area once lay beneath the sea and is extremely fertile. There's also an area of tidal saltmarsh, enclosed in the early 19th century for grazing cattle.

the ride

1 The car park marks the site of the old Braunton railway station, closed in 1965. The line – Barnstaple to Ilfracombe – was opened in 1874, and the last train ran in 1970. Cycle to the far end of the **car park** and turn right into the overflow area. Bear left and leave the car park by the police station (right). Bear right onto Station Road and cycle down it, passing the cycle hire on the left. Turn right into **Station Close** and then immediately left down a tarmac way. At the end cross the lane; keep ahead through black bollards to cross another lane, with a roundabout right.

On the Tarka Trail

2 Follow signs left to pick up the **old railway line**. Pass a wetland conservation area (left) and pass round a staggered barrier to cross a lane (the wire fences right mark the boundary of RAF Chivenor).

3 (Note: For The Williams Arms turn left here; at the end of the lane cross the A361 with care; the pub is on the other side.) Cycle on to reach a roundabout at the entrance to **RAF Chivenor**. The church ahead left is St Augustine's at Heanton Punchardon, built by Richard Punchardon (owner of Heanton estate) after his return from the Crusades in 1290. The village, formerly Heanton (Saxon Hantona – High Town) took on his name from that time. Cross the road by the roundabout and keep ahead through a wooded section.

4 Emerge suddenly from woodland onto the **Taw Estuary**, with far-reaching views. Listen for the oystercatcher's piping call, and watch out for curlew, easily identified by its curving bill. In winter thousands of migrant birds feed on the broad sandbanks here. Pass castellated **Heanton Court** on the left, a refuge for Royalists in the Civil War. The then owner of the Heanton estate, Colonel Albert Basset, fought for Barnstaple, which eventually fell to the Parliamentarians. Continue along the banks of the Taw to pass the **football club** (left).

5 Cross arched **Yeo Bridge**, a swing bridge over a tributary of the Taw, and pass the **Civic Centre** on the left (cyclists and pedestrians separate here). Bear left away from the river to meet the road. Turn right

MAP: OS Explorer 139 Bideford, Ilfracombe & Barnstaple

START/FINISH: Braunton car park (contributions), grid ref: SS486365

TRAILS/TRACKS: level tarmac and gritty former railway track

LANDSCAPE: townscape, estuary

PUBLIC TOILETS: at start and in Barnstaple

TOURIST INFORMATION: Barnstaple, tel 01271 375000

CYCLE HIRE: Otter Cycle Hire, tel 01271 813339; Tarka Trail Cycle Hire, Barnstaple, tel 01271 324202

THE PUB: The Williams Arms, Wrafton

! Busy crossing of A361 on route to the Williams Arms

Getting to the start

Braunton lies on the A361 Barnstaple to Ilfracombe road in north Devon. The car park is signed from the traffic lights in the centre of the village. If approaching from Barnstaple, turn left, and 100yds (91m) later turn left into the car park.

Why do this cycle ride?

Visiting Barnstaple by car at the height of the tourist season can be something of a trial as this north Devon market town, the oldest borough in the country, can get pretty choked by traffic. So what better way to get into the heart of Barnstaple than by cycling from Braunton via the Tarka Trail along the edge of the Taw estuary?

Researched and written by: Sue Viccars

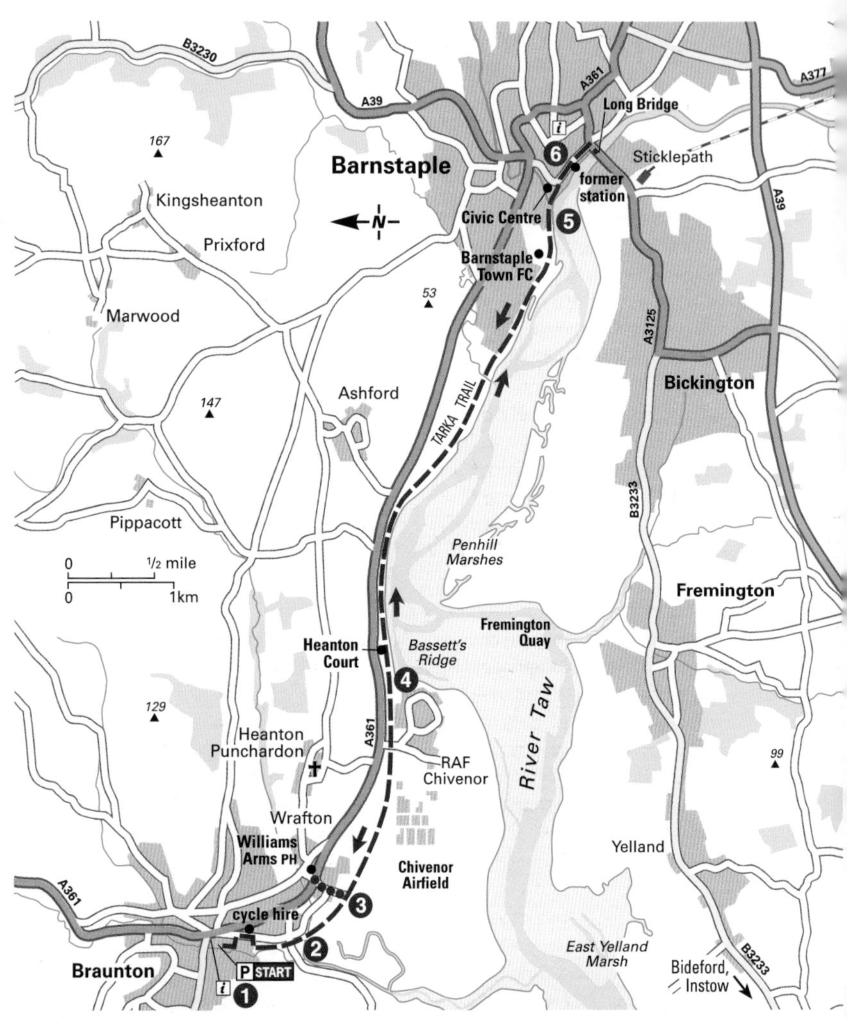

along the cycle path past **old Barnstaple Town Station** on the right (the railway reached the south side of the river in 1854, and this side in the early 1870s). Bear right as signed, then left along the **quay** (note: there is no wall along the edge).

6 Continue on to pass **Barnstaple Heritage Centre** (left), with its elaborate statue of Queen Anne. The Riverside Café (with cycle racks) lies a few yards along on the left, just before Barnstaple's Long Bridge over the Taw (there has been a bridge here since the 13th century). There is evidence of a settlement at Barnstaple from early Saxon times; trade via the Taw was vital to the town's prosperity for centuries. Queen Anne's Walk marks the site of the Great and Little Quays, once bustling with ocean-going ships, including five bound for Sir Francis Drake's Armada fleet in 1588.

The Williams Arms

6

A modernised thatched village pub that is well worth the short diversion off the trail. It is really geared up to family dining and has the added attraction of a children's play area in its spacious garden. Popular with both holidaymakers and locals, the two huge bars have been smartly refurbished with plush red carpets, a mix of modern furnishings and a self-service carvery, yet they retain some character in the form of low-beamed ceilings and open fires. Separate games area with pool table, darts and TV.

Food

The lounge bar menu offers a good choice of filled rolls and paninis, ploughman's lunches with home-cooked ham or local cheddar, steaks from the grill, and specialities like steak and venison pie, Exmoor venison braised in red wine and brandy, roast duck with orange sauce, and roast meats from the daily carvery.

Family facilities

Children are welcome thoughout the pub. It is really geared to family dining and you'll find a games/TV room, a basic kid's menu, smaller portions for older children, high chairs, and a play fort in the large garden.

about the pub

The Williams Arms
Wrafton, Braunton
Devon EX33 2DE
Tel 01271 812360
www.williams-arms.co.uk

DIRECTIONS: the pub is beside the A361 Braunton to Barnstaple road, 1 mile (1.6km) south east of Braunton. See Point 3

PARKING: 100

OPEN: daily; all day

FOOD: daily

BREWERY/COMPANY: free house

REAL ALE: Bass

Alternative refreshment stops

There are plenty of pubs and cafés in Braunton and Barnstaple, and en route you'll find Heanton Court, another family-friendly pub.

☛ Where to go from here

On the edge of Exmoor at Blackmoor Gate is the Exmoor Zoological Park, which specialises in smaller animals, many of which are endangered species, such as the golden headed lion tamarins. There are contact pens and children are encouraged to participate (www.exmoorzoo.co.uk). Combe Martin Wildlife Park and Dinosaur Park is a subtropical paradise which has hundreds of birds and animals and some animatronic dinosaurs, plus there are sea lion shows, falconry displays and animal handling sessions (www.dinosaur-park.com).

7

The Tarka Trail – Instow to Barnstaple

Fremington Quay
There's little evidence at Fremington Quay today to suggest that in the mid 19th century this was said to be the busiest port between Land's End and Bristol. The deepwater quay was built in the 1840s (with a horse-drawn rail link to Barnstaple), when silting of the River Taw prevented large ships from going further upriver. Before that time a local port operated from Fremington Pill, which the trail crosses en route for Fremington Quay. The main exports were clay and minerals, the main imports coal and limestone from south Wales for burning in local limekilns. The quay received another boost to its fortunes in 1854 when the mainline railway reached Barnstaple, and led to further development of the line to Bideford, which opened to passengers in late 1855. Exports of clay – from as far away as Peters Marland, 16 miles (25.7km) away – continued until the early 20th century.

The railway was closed in the 1960s, and the quay was taken out of use in 1969. Today the café and heritage centre, which opened in 2001, are housed in the reconstructed station building and signal box. There are picnic tables outside the café with lovely views across the Taw. The decline of shipping in the estuary, and the disappearance of local railways, has had a beneficial effect on local flora and fauna.

the ride

1 Turn left out of the car park and cycle along Marine Parade, passing **The Bar Inn** on the left. At the restored signal box (it was built in the early 1870s) turn left onto the **old railway line**.

2 The trail runs through a long cutting before emerging through an area of **wooden chalets**, with views left across dunes to the junction of the Torridge and Taw rivers, with the southern end of the sand dunes at Braunton Burrows beyond. Pass the **cricket ground** left, and then a picnic area and car park.

3 Continue over the access road to a **small industrial area** and then you're right out in the open. Pass East Yelland and Home Farm marshes and then the RSPB's **Isley Marsh reserve**, a saltmarsh habitat and high-tide roost. A short run through a wooded cutting leads to the viaduct over Fremington Pill – look left to see a limekiln – and **Fremington Quay**.

4 The trail (now tarmac) passes in front of the café, then bears right past a parking and **picnic area** (left) and through a wooded cutting. A long embanked stretch leads all the way to Barnstaple. Penhill Marshes (jutting out into the estuary just east of Fremington Quay) have been reclaimed for grazing livestock. Along the trail you'll spot the 'creeps' – tunnels through the embankment enable cattle to access drier land at times of high tide. The large expanses of saltmarsh and mudflats along the estuary provide important habitats for a wide range of highly specialised plants and wildlife. Oystercatcher and redshank, among many other species, overwinter here. In late summer look out for the golden flowers of the sea aster, one of the few plants that can cope with being submerged by saltwater, and which helps to stabilise the marshes. In the cuttings either side of the Quay see if you can spot blue field

A *Sustrans milepost on the Tarka Trail*

7

MAP: OS Explorer 139 Bideford, Ilfracombe & Barnstaple

START/FINISH: Instow car park (fee-paying), grid ref: SS472303

TRAILS/TRACKS: level tarmac and gritty former railway track

LANDSCAPE: townscape, estuary

PUBLIC TOILETS: Instow; Fremington Quay

TOURIST INFORMATION: Barnstaple, tel 01271 375000

CYCLE HIRE: Biketrail, Fremington Quay, tel 01271 372586; Bideford Cycle Hire, East-the-Water, tel 01237 424123

THE PUB: The Bar Inn, Instow

! Fremington Quay is very busy with bikes and people at peak holiday times

Getting to the start

Instow lies on the Torridge Estuary, signed off the B3233 Barnstaple to Bideford road. Approaching from Barnstaple, take the second sign right. From Bideford, take the first sign left. Pass The Bar Inn on the right and the car park in about 100yds (91m).

Why do this cycle ride?

This second chunk of the Tarka Trail can be linked with either the route from Torrington to Bideford, or that from Braunton to Barnstaple. It stands on its own, however, as an easy ride from the delightful village of Instow along the southern side of the Taw Estuary to Barnstaple, passing historic Fremington Quay.

Researched and written by: Sue Viccars

scabious in summer, and spotted meadow brown butterflies feeding on its flowers. The trail narrows as the edge of **Sticklepath** (opposite Barnstaple) is reached: cyclists are asked to give way to pedestrians.

5 Where the road bridge (A3125) can be seen ahead, bear left for 20yds (18m). At the next junction bear left for the **Long Bridge** if you want to go into Barnstaple; if not, retrace your route to the cricket ground (see Point 2).

6 Just after the entrance to the ground, turn right on a narrow path as signed for the Wayfarer Inn and **beach café**. Meet a track running through the dunes and turn left, passing the café on the right. Emerge onto the road and keep ahead along the seafront, to find the car park on the left. This alternative return gives lovely views over **the Torridge** towards the attractive fishing village of Appledore, an important port in Elizabethan times. During the 18th century Bideford and Appledore were the largest importers of tobacco in the country; today Appledore is famous for its shipbuilding tradition. Much of the village's network of narrow streets and cobbled courtyards is a conservation area; catch the ferry from Instow Quay for a closer look.

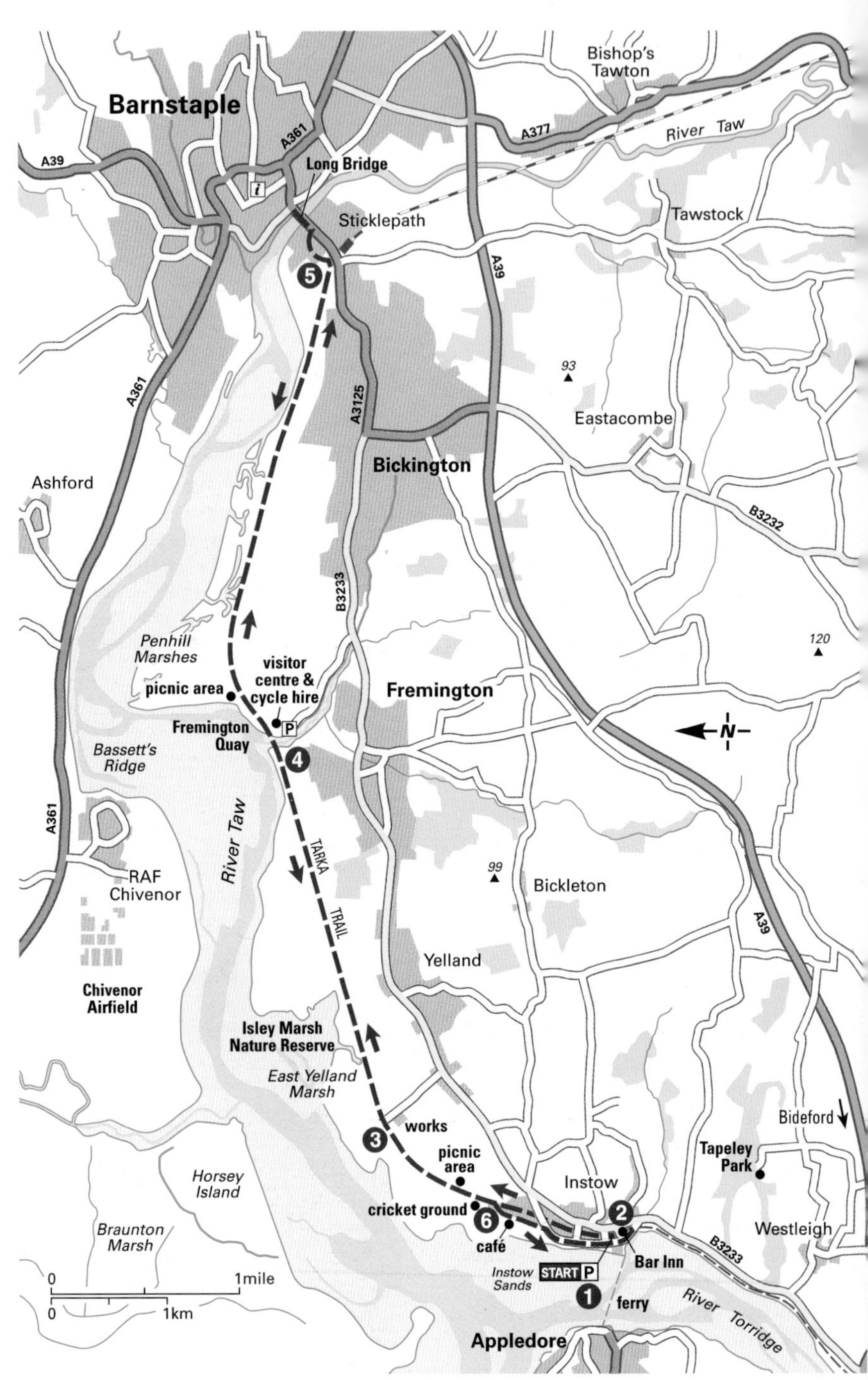
Barnstaple
Bishop's Tawton
A377
River Taw
A39
A361
Long Bridge
Sticklepath
Tawstock
A39
93
Eastacombe
A3125
A361
Bickington
Ashford
B3232
B3233
Penhill Marshes
120
visitor centre & cycle hire
picnic area
Fremington
Fremington Quay
Bassett's Ridge
A361
River Taw
TARKA TRAIL
99
Bickleton
RAF Chivenor
A39
Yelland
Chivenor Airfield
Isley Marsh Nature Reserve
East Yelland Marsh
works
Bideford
Tapeley Park
picnic area
Horsey Island
Instow
cricket ground
café
Westleigh
Braunton Marsh
Bar Inn
B3233
Instow Sands
START
ferry
River Torridge
0
1mile
0
1km
Appledore

The Bar Inn

Lively and interesting little pub situated right on the quay with super views across the estuary from waterside tables outside the pub. The interior is rustic, open-plan and full of character, attracting a mixed clientele, from local fishermen and holidaymakers to walkers and cyclists on the Tarka Trail in search of refreshment. Locally brewed beers, perhaps Jollyboat ales from Bideford or Barum ales from Barnstaple, are particularly popular, as are the summer afternoon teas.

Food

The bar menu is huge, offering something for everyone, from crusty baguettes and crab salad to breaded plaice, fish pie, salmon and prawn fishcakes, and lamb shank with mash and rosemary gravy. Daily specials include fresh local fish like sea bass and plaice.

Family facilities

Although there is no family room children are welcome in the pub. There are high chairs, special meals for younger children and smaller portions are available.

Alternative refreshment stops

There are plenty of pubs, cafés and restaurants to choose from in Barnstaple. There's a café at the old station at Fremington Quay and the New Inn in Fremington.

☛ Where to go from here

Appeldore is home to the North Devon Maritime Museum where you can learn about the ship and boat building industry and the maritime activities of the area. Youngsters will love the Gnome Reserve and Wildflower Garden near Bradworthy (www.gnomereserve.co.uk), and the exhilarating rides and shows at the Milky Way Adventure Park near Clovelly (www.themilkyway.co.uk). Equally fascinating is the Quince Honey Farm at South Molton where you can follow the story of honey and beeswax from flower to table, as well as see the world of bees close up and in complete safety (www.quincehoney.co.uk).

about the pub

The Bar Inn
Marine Parade, Instow
Bideford, Devon EX39 4HY
Tel 01271 860624

DIRECTIONS: see Getting to the start
PARKING: 8, nearby
OPEN: daily; all day
FOOD: daily
BREWERY/COMPANY: free house
REAL ALE: Doom Bar, Dartmoor

The Tarka Trail – Great Torrington to Bideford

Tarka the Otter

The Tarka Trail is named after the hero of north Devon, author Henry Williamson's famous novel *Tarka the Otter*, published in 1927. Williamson moved to Georgeham, near Braunton, in 1921, having visited the area in 1914, at which time he became captivated by this remote part of north Devon. He came here both to recover from the horrors of active service in World War I and also to write, and between 1921 and 1972 almost 50 works were published. His best known is the tale of Tarka the Otter, much of which is based around the River Torridge, which flows northwest for 9 miles (14.5km) from its source to its junction with the River Taw just beyond Appledore. Tarka was born just below Canal Bridge, downstream from Torrington, and met his end on the River Torridge too. The story was made into a film and, by strange coincidence, Williamson died on the same day as the filming of Tarka's death scene, in 1977. It seems fitting that today, after many years of decline, otters are returning to Devon's rivers as a result of deliberate policy to improve habitat and water quality.

the ride

1 Turn right along the A386 and descend to pick up the Tarka Trail on the right before **Rolle Bridge**. It runs between The Puffing Billy – the old station building – and cycle hire in the goods yard opposite. Turn left along the trail to pass the pub and garden (cycle racks) on the left. The railway reached Bideford (from Barnstaple) in 1855; the extension (under the London and South Western Railway) from Bideford to Torrington opened July 1872, and closed in the mid 1960s. The 'Atlantic Coast Express' ran from here all the way to London Waterloo. Cycle over the **River Torridge** as it loops its way towards the sea.

2 Pause at the next river crossing to look at **Beam Weir**; as you cross the river for the third time look left towards Beam Aqueduct. Part of the railway utilised the bed of the former Rolle Canal, and was involved in a scheme to link with the Bude Canal in north Cornwall; only a 6-mile (9.7km) section was completed, in 1827. Lime and coal were carried inland from the

A fisherman on the River Torridge where Henry Williamson set his novel Tarka the Otter

coast to Torrington, and agricultural produce exported. Pass a **picnic area** left, and continue between the A386 and the Torridge (right). Look right through the trees towards Weare Giffard, with its 14th-century church and 15th-century manor house. Pass **Weare Giffard Cross** (left).

3 Where the Torridge takes a wide loop east cycle through **Landcross Tunnel** (lit), then through a cutting by Landcross Bridge. Now with the River Yeo on the left, cycle on to meet the **old iron railway bridge** over the Torridge.

4 The whole feel of the route changes here: the river is wide and slow, with large expanses of saltmarsh and reedbed, home to sedge warbler and reed bunting, and beautiful views. The bridge overlooks the 'Pool of the Six Herons' (mentioned in *Tarka*) – look out for herons, lapwing, redshank and curlew. Saltmarsh plants (specially adapted to seawater inundations) and reedbeds protect the river banks from erosion, and the mudflats support millions of invertebrates, food for wading birds. Limestone was shipped in from south Wales for burning in the limekiln left of the bridge; local woodland supplied timber for charcoal.

5 Continue along the right bank of the Torridge, with increasingly good views of **Bideford**, a significant port in medieval times, today a busy market town and

8

2h30 · 11 MILES · 17.7 KM · LEVEL 123

MAP: OS Explorer 126 Clovelly & Hartland

START/FINISH: car park on Great Torrington Common, grid ref: SS485193

TRAILS/TRACKS: level former railway track, now smooth tarmac

LANDSCAPE: woodland, river and estuary, saltmarsh, townscape

PUBLIC TOILETS: near Bideford station

TOURIST INFORMATION: Bideford, tel 01237 477676

CYCLE HIRE: Torridge Cycle Hire, Station Yard, tel 01805 622633; Bideford Cycle Hire, East-the-Water, tel 01237 4241123

THE PUB: The Puffing Billy, Great Torrington

Getting to the start

From Great Torrington take the A386 Bideford road across Great Torrington Common. Use the car park on the common opposite the junction with the B3227.

Why do this cycle ride?

The Tarka Trail, a 180-mile (290km) cycleway and footpath, offers great opportunities for exploring north Devon. The trail opened in May 1992, and those sections along former railway lines make great cycling routes. This ride from Great Torrington to Bideford, along the broad banks of the River Torridge, is one of three options, and can easily be linked to the route from Instow to Barnstaple.

Researched and written by: Sue Viccars

8

working port. Its 24-arched stone bridge recalls the town's early prosperity – it is said that each arch was funded by a local parish, and the size of the arch reflects their respective wealth! The 19th-century novelist Charles Kingsley (who lived at Clovelly during his childhood) described Bideford as 'the Little White Town that slopes upward from its broad river tide': little has changed.

6 Turn-around point is **old Bideford Station** – 220.5 miles (355km) from Waterloo! The Tarka Trail goes on to Instow. Refreshments are available from the **Railway Carriage Visitor Centre**. If you have time when you finish the ride, take a look around Great Torrington, noted for the Battle of Great Torrington in 1646. This battle marked the end of Royalist resistance in the West Country in the Civil War.

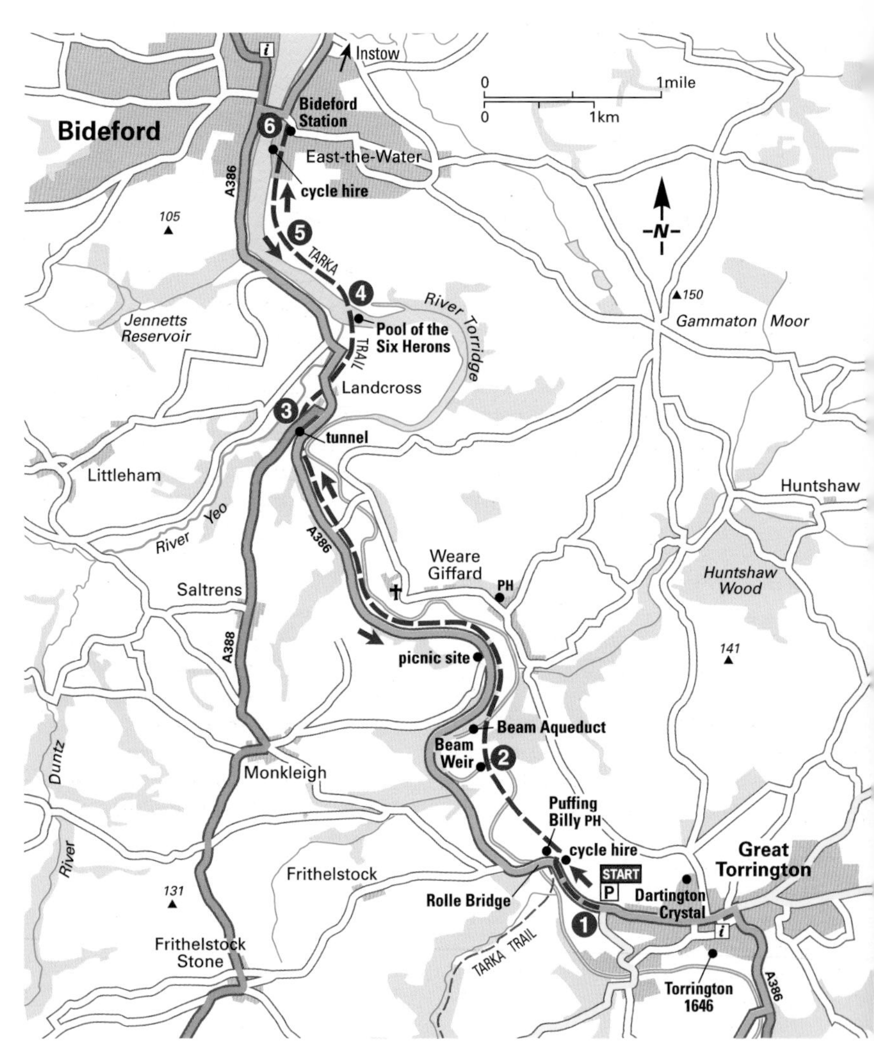

Torrington DEVON

The Puffing Billy

Smack beside the former railway route and looking every inch the old station building it once was, the Puffing Billy is gradually being restored and makes the ideal post-ride refreshment stop on this section of the Tarka Trail. On fine days you can relax in the trail-side garden with a pint of locally-brewed Cavalier ale. There's a real sense of history inside due to the mass of authentic railway and station memorabilia that fills the atmospheric bars, including the original signs and platform notices used at the station.

about the pub

The Puffing Billy
Station Hill, Great Torrington
Devon EX38 8JD
Tel 01805 623050

DIRECTIONS: right off the A386 1 mile (1.6km) west of Great Torrington, just before Rolle Bridge over the River Torridge

PARKING: 30

OPEN: daily; all day Easter to October; closed Wednesdays November to Easter

FOOD: daily

BREWERY/COMPANY: Burrington Brewery

REAL ALE: Puffing Billy and Opus ales

Food

They open at 11am and you can call in during the morning for a reviving cup of coffee. On the daytime menu you'll find baguettes and ploughman's lunches, ham, egg and chips, and steak and kidney pie. Specials may take in lasagne, spaghetti carbonara and mixed grills, and a separate menu is served in the Station Restaurant.

Family facilities

The pub is very child friendly; they are welcome everywhere and there's a children's menu and a garden.

Alternative refreshment stops

There's a good choice of pubs and cafés in Bideford, including at Bideford old station, your turn-around point.

☛ Where to go from here

Take a fascinating factory tour at Dartington Crystal in Great Torrington and watch craftsmen transform hot molten crystal into elegant glassware from the safety of elevated viewing galleries. Children can have fun in the glass activity area and you can discover the story of glass and the history of Dartington at the Visitor Centre (www.dartington.co.uk). Stroll down the steep cobbled street of Clovelly, one of Devon's most famous coastal villages, or visit the Milky Way Adventure Park to experience some exhilarating rides and shows (www.themilkyway.co.uk). Another family attraction – The Big Sheep (www.thebigsheep.co.uk) – is close to Bideford.

9

Okehampton DEVON

The Granite Way

A glorious, easy ride along an old railway line around the northwestern edge of Dartmoor, with an optional hilly extension to Bridestowe and historic Lydford.

Okehampton Castle and Lydford Gorge

The atmospheric ruins of Okehampton's Norman castle – once the largest in Devon – peep through the trees north of the line near the start of this ride. Built soon after the Norman Conquest, most of what can be seen today dates from the 13th and 15th centuries. The castle – seat of the Earls of Devon in medieval times – is beautifully situated on the banks of the West Okement River, with walks and picnic areas near by. It lies at one end of the Two Castles Trail, a 24-mile (39km) walking route linking it with the Norman castle at Launceston in east Cornwall.

At the other end of the ride lies Lydford, once an administrative centre for the Forest of Dartmoor. Lydford Castle, a tower built in the late 12th century as a prison and courtroom, was used by the Royalists in the Civil War. There's also the National Trust's Lydford Gorge. During the Ice Age the River Lyd carved a new and tortuous route through solid rock as it coursed west towards the River Tavy. The waters now hurtle through the 1.5 mile- (2.4km) long gorge via a succession of waterfalls and pools, including the beautiful 98ft (30m) White Lady waterfall. Various paths, some narrow and slippery, wend their way through the surrounding oak woodlands.

the ride

1 From Okehampton Station cross **Station Road** and keep ahead, as signed, parallel to the railway. After 50yds (46m) turn left onto a tarmac way that then bears right to run parallel to the railway. Follow this as it bears left under a bridge. Continue on to pass through a gate, left under the A30, through another gate, and right on the other side. The route bears away from the railway to reach **Meldon Quarry**, which started 200 years ago to produce a variety of materials, including 'Hornfells' used in construction work, and which was exposed when the railway cuttings were dug.

2 The next stop is **old Meldon Station** with its visitor centre. There's a buffet in a couple of old railway carriages, and a picnic area, with glorious views over Meldon's steel viaduct and towards Dartmoor's highest ground. The Devon and Cornwall Railway reached Okehampton in 1871 and was absorbed into the London and South Western Railway the following year. The line was extended to Lydford via the viaduct (which soars 150ft/46m over the West Okement Valley) in 1874, and

closed to commercial passenger traffic in 1968. Today the 'Dartmoor Pony' runs out here from Okehampton on weekends and during the summer holidays.

3 Continue on over the **viaduct** – a fantastic ride, but take care in high winds (for Meldon Reservoir leave the route left just after the viaduct; on reaching the lane go straight over). Pass through a long cutting on the edge of **Prewley Moor**, after which views open up towards Sourton Tor (unusually formed of basalt, not granite). Cross the access lane to **Prewley Works**, and pass the pretty church of St Thomas à Becket at Sourton. The Highwayman pub can be accessed over the A386 here. Continue on through a short gated section at **Albrae**, and on past ponds to reach **Lake Viaduct**, built of local stone in 1874, and more lovely views.

4 Here you have a choice. The line ends 0.75 mile (1.2km) further on at **Southerly Halt picnic site**, so you can cycle on and turn round there. If you want to go either to **The Bearslake Inn,** or on to Lydford, turn left off the track just after the viaduct and descend steeply to a gate. Turn

9

4h00 — 18 MILES — 29 KM — LEVEL 123 (3)

SHORTER ALTERNATIVE ROUTE

2h15 — 11 MILES — 17.7 KM — LEVEL 123 (1)

MAP: OS Explorer OL28 Dartmoor

START/FINISH: Okehampton Station, grid ref: SX591944

TRAILS/TRACKS: level tarmac track, rough bridlepath to Bearslake Inn, narrow lanes/level track to Lydford

LANDSCAPE: moorland edge, farmland, woodland

PUBLIC TOILETS: at start and in Lydford

TOURIST INFORMATION: Okehampton, tel 01837 53020

CYCLE HIRE: YHA, Okehampton Station, tel 01837 53916

THE PUB: The Bearslake Inn, Lake

! Crossing of A386 on Lydford extension, steep descent/ascent into/out of Bridestowe

Getting to the start

Okehampton lies off the A30 on the northern edge of Dartmoor. Make your way to the town centre and follow signs for the railway station.

Why do this cycle ride?

There are so many options on this ride that it's hard to know which to recommend! It really is a route to suit all tastes and abilities. Quite apart from traversing stunningly beautiful landscapes, there are several possible picnic and refreshment stops along the way. Keen cyclists can extend the route via quiet country lanes to rejoin the old railway line and continue on to Lydford.

Researched and written by: Sue Viccars

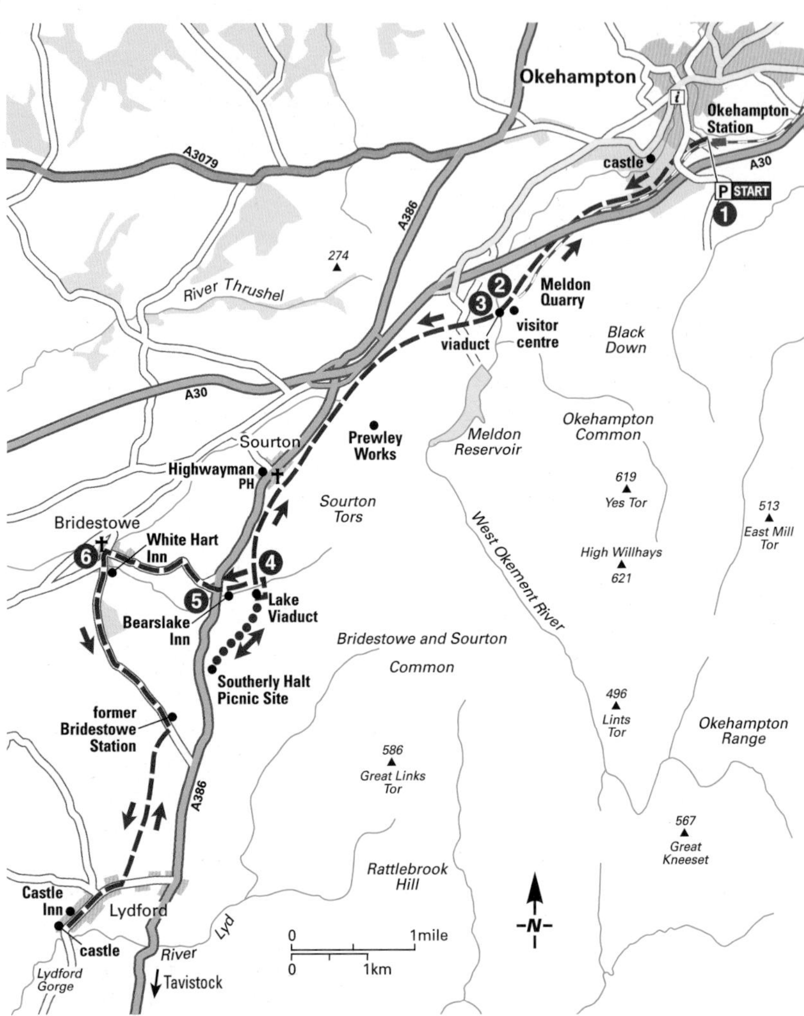

left under the **viaduct** and follow this rough track downhill to meet the A396. Turn left into the grounds of the pub, originally a 13th-century longhouse.

5 To continue to the ancient Saxon burgh of Lydford, cross the A386 – take great care – and cycle up the quiet lane opposite. At the T-junction turn left and follow the lane downhill into **Bridestowe**.

6 Turn left opposite the church, passing the White Hart Inn on the left. Cycle up Station Road (steep) and follow this for 1.5 miles (2.4km) to **old Bridestowe Station**. Cross the bridge and turn right onto the old railway track again. Follow this to Lydford. Leave the track and turn right down the road for the Castle Inn, castle and **Lydford Gorge**. Retrace your route back to Okehampton.

The Bearslake Inn

9

Standing on the edge of the National Park and built as a farm in the 13th century, this thatched and stone-built Devon longhouse is conveniently located beside the Granite Way cycle trail. Oozing old-world charm and character, expect to find flagstone floors, exposed beams and timbers, head-crackingly low ceilings, old pews, and a fine inglenook fireplace with crackling log fire in the rambling interior. Food is freshly prepared on the premises using local produce, including fish landed at Plymouth Quay and Taw Valley cheeses. Cyclists are very welcome and there's plenty of space in both the front and rear gardens to rest and relax on fine summer days.

about the pub

The Bearslake Inn
Lake, Sourton, Okehampton
Devon EX20 4HQ
Tel: 01837 861334
www.bearslakeinn.com

DIRECTIONS: pub is situated north of Lydford on the A386 Okehampton to Tavistock road
PARKING: 40
OPEN: daily, closed Sun evening
FOOD: daily
BREWERY/COMPANY: free house
REAL ALE: Otter, Teignworth, Cottleigh, St Austell plus changing guest beers
ROOMS: 6 en suite

Food

Lunchtime snacks take in filled baguettes, open and closed sandwiches, old favourites such as freshly cooked three-egg omelettes, local ham, egg and chips and a selection of vegetarian meals. Imaginative evening meals in the upmarket Stables restaurant feature West Country meat, fish and cheese in a variety of dishes which change regularly.

Family facilities

Although children are not allowed in the bar there are two family dining areas. Smaller portions are available and children are welcome overnight.

Alternative refreshment stops

Plenty of pubs and cafés in Okehampton and the eccentric Highwayman Inn at Sourton. If continuing to Lydford, you'll pass the White Hart in Bridestow and the Castle Inn in Lydford.

☛ Where to go from here

Discover how people lived, worked and played on and around Dartmoor at the Museum of Dartmoor Life in Okehampton, housed on three floors in a 19th-century mill (www.museumofdartmoorlife.co.uk). Visit Okehampton Castle and enjoy the free audio tour which brings this romantic ruin to life (www.english-heritage.org.uk). Daily demonstrations at the Finch Foundry Working Museum in Sticklepath show how water-powered hammers made sickles, scythes and other hand tools. In Lydford, explore the spectacular gorge formed by the River Lyd (www.nationaltrust.org.uk), and look round Lydford Castle, a 12th-century tower that was once a notorious prison.

Around the quarries of Princetown

A tough ride through the wilds of Dartmoor, along the old route of the Princetown to Yelverton railway.

Quarrying round Princetown

There's a long history of quarrying granite on Dartmoor. Quarrying began around 1820 at both Haytor Quarry, under George Templer, and (in direct competition) at Swelltor and Foggintor, under Thomas Trywhitt (who also built roads and many buildings in the Princetown area, including the Plume of Feathers Inn in 1785). Foggintor (originally known as Royal Oak) ceased working around 1900, and Swelltor in 1921. Both reopened for a while in 1937, in response to an increase in demand for roadstone. Foggintor supplied granite for Dartmoor Prison, and local granite was also used in Nelson's Column in Trafalgar Square, London. Look towards Foggintor (Point 3) and you'll see various ruined buildings: as well as cottages, there was also a chapel used as a school. The old quarry workings are now flooded and provide a peaceful picnic spot.

Merrivale Quarry (originally Tor Quarry), a little further along the route, was the last working quarry on Dartmoor, operating from 1875 to 1997. Granite blocks from the

1h45 | 5 MILES | 8 KM | LEVEL 123

old London Bridge were re-dressed here when the bridge was sold to the USA, and stone was also used in the war memorial in the Falklands after the war in 1982.

the ride

1 Turn left out of the car park along the rough road. Just past the **fire station** (left) bear left as signposted (disused railway/Tyrwhitt Trail) on a narrow fenced path, which bears right. Go through a gate. The path widens to a gritty track, and passes a **coniferous plantation** (right).

2 Suddenly you're out in the open on a long embankment, looking towards the forests around **Burrator Reservoir** ahead right, below **Sheeps Tor** (left) and **Sharpitor** (right). Continue along the contours of the hill – it's quite rough – as you progress look ahead left to the railway winding its way towards **Ingra Tor**. This is the old Plymouth and Dartmoor railway line, brainchild of Sir Thomas Tyrwhitt, friend of and private secretary to the Prince Regent. Originally a tramway with horse-drawn wagons, it opened in 1823. It was part of Tyrwhitt's plans to exploit the area's natural resources (granite), at the same time enabling materials such as coal and lime to be brought to Princetown more easily. The Princetown Railway Company (a subsidiary of the GWR) took it over in 1881; it reopened as a steam railway in 1883, but was never profitable and closed in 1956. However, it's a great footpath and cycle track.

Top: The Dartmoor Inn at Merrivale Bridge
Left: Walkers on the trail

MAP: OS Explorer OL28 Dartmoor

START/FINISH: Princetown car park (contributions), grid ref: SX588735

TRAILS/TRACKS: rocky former railway track and one particularly steep and rough section

LANDSCAPE: open moorland

PUBLIC TOILETS: at start

TOURIST INFORMATION: High Moorland Visitor Centre, Princetown, tel 01822 890414

CYCLE HIRE: Runnage Farm, Postbridge (plus camping barn), tel 01822 880222

THE PUB: Dartmoor Inn, near Princetown

! Only suitable for older children with mountain bikes

Getting to the start

Princetown lies on the B3212 between Two Bridges and Yelverton, on Dartmoor. From Two Bridges, turn right in the middle of the town; from Yelverton, turn left (High Moorland Visitor Centre on the corner), following signs for the car park.

Why do this cycle ride?

This is a rather different sort of ride, and one that will test both your bike and your concentration! It follows the line of the old Princetown to Yelverton railway, but has not been surfaced. It's suitable for families with older children and those who have mountain bikes, and you'll have to push your bikes up one particularly rough section. But for a taste of Dartmoor 'proper', it's hard to beat.

Researched and written by: Sue Viccars

3 Reach the edge of **Foggintor Quarry** (left), with Swelltor Quarry on the hill ahead; a track crosses the trail. The site of King Tor Halt (1928), from where a siding led to Foggintor, is near by. Keep straight ahead, almost immediately taking the left fork (the track becomes grassier). Look right towards the spoil heaps of Foggintor Quarry. Follow the track on – look left towards Merrivale Quarry (the Dartmoor Inn is just out of sight below) – try to spot the Bronze Age **Merrivale stone rows**. Follow the track as it bears left round the hill (below King's Tor Quarry), to enjoy views right over **Vixen Tor**, almost 100ft (30m) high, home to one of the moor's most evil characters, the witch Vixana. Pass through a cutting – another branch joins right – and keep on to another fork.

4 Keep right along the lower track; views change again, with the wooded **Walkham Valley** below right and – on a good day – the sparkling waters of Plymouth Sound in the distance. About 50yds (46m) beyond the fork look left to see a pile of dressed stone on the upper track: 12 granite corbels, cut in 1903 for work on London Bridge, but excess to requirements. Pass the spoil heaps of **Swelltor Quarry**; the track is now fenced on the right, with views ahead to the bridge en route for **Ingra Tor**.

5 Where the track starts to curve sharp right, turn left opposite an old gate. Push your bike up a rough, rocky track to regain the outward route near **Foggintor Quarry**.

6 Turn right and make your way bumpily back to **Princetown**. The building of the infamous prison in 1806 – originally for French prisoners from the Napoleonic wars – was also down to Trywhitt. Since 1850 it has been a civilian establishment.

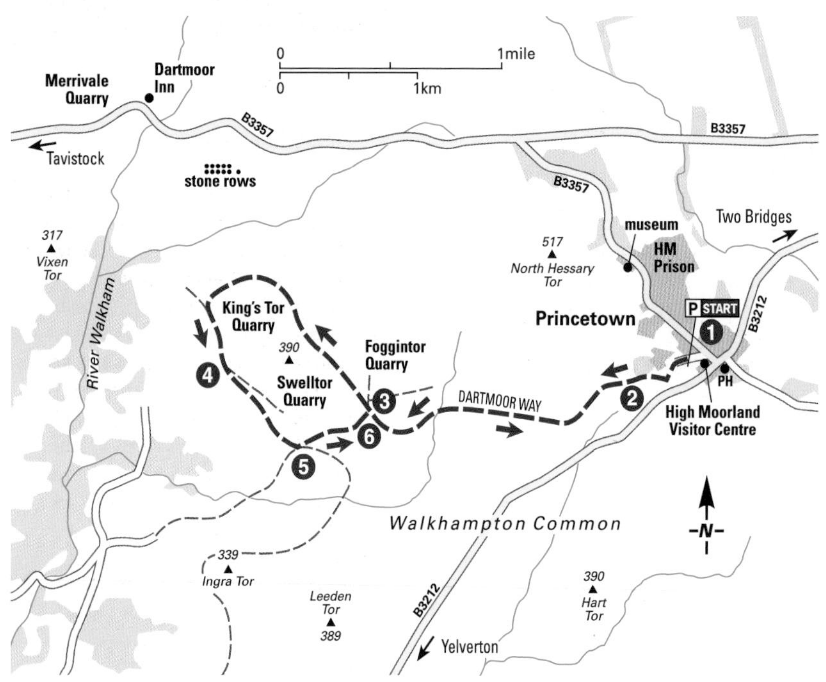

Dartmoor Inn

10

Situated at 1,000ft (305m) above sea level, this whitewashed old inn enjoys sweeping views across moorland and the Walkham Valley, and on a clear evening the lights of Plymouth and the Eddystone Lighthouse can be seen. Originally quarryman's cottages built in the 17th century, the pub was once part of the Walreddon Manor Estate and has been a pub since at least 1852. A roaring log fire in a big stone fireplace is a welcome sight in the largely open-plan and partly carpeted main bar. On fine summer days soak up the view with a pint at one of the picnic benches on the grassy area to the front of the pub.

Food

Traditional bar meals range from salads, ploughman's and filled baps, to chicken, ham and mushroom pie, gammon steak and jam sponge and custard. Evening dishes take in grills, pasta meals and specialities like rack of lamb and steak au poivre.

Family facilities

Although there are no special facilities for children, families are made very welcome.

Alternative refreshment stops

There are pubs and tea rooms to be found in Princetown.

about the pub

Dartmoor Inn
Merrivale Bridge, Princetown
Devon PL20 6ST
Tel: 01822 890340

DIRECTIONS: load up bikes, turn left out of the car park, pass the prison and turn left again at the T-junction with the B3357, the pub is on the right in 1.5 miles (3km)

PARKING: 25

OPEN: closed Sunday evening, Monday and Tuesday between November and Easter

FOOD: daily

BREWERY/COMPANY: free house

REAL ALE: Marston's Pedigree, Bass, guest beer

ROOMS: 4 bedrooms, 2 en suite

☛ Where to go from here

To discover more about the history of Dartmoor, and what to see and do in the area, visit the High Moorland Visitor Centre in Princetown (www.dartmoor-npa.gov.uk). Young children will enjoy a visit to Dartmoor's Miniature Pony and Animal Farm near Moretonhampstead, where they can see ponies, donkeys, pigs and lambs at close quarters, and there are nature trails and indoor and outdoor play areas (www.miniatureponycentre.com). Discover the rugged beauty of the Bovey Valley at the Becky Falls Woodland Park (www.beckyfalls-dartmoor.com), and the world of otters and butterflies at the fascinating Buckfast Butterfly Farm and Dartmoor Otter Sanctuary (www.ottersandbutterflies.co.uk).

The Plym Valley Trail

A pleasant ride along the line of the old Plym Valley railway, with an optional extension to the National Trust's magnificent house and parkland at Saltram.

Plym Bridge Woods and Blaxton Meadow

This railway line opened in 1859 under the South Devon and Tavistock Railway, and ran for 16 miles (25.7km) from Plymouth to Tavistock. The cycle route through Plym Bridge Woods is one of the best bits. The woods became popular with daytrippers who alighted at Plym Bridge Halt, built in 1906 (on the site of the car park mentioned in Point 5). You'll also see evidence of industrial activity: there were several quarries here, workers' cottages, a small lead/silver mine, a canal and three railway lines. The remains of 18th-century Rumple Quarry – from which slate was extracted – and engine house are passed on the right, soon after entering the woods. Plym Bridge Woods are particularly lovely in spring, thick with wood anenomes, primroses, bluebells and ransoms.

Once in the Saltram estate you soon pass Blaxton Meadow on your right, an area of managed saltmarsh on the Plym Estuary. It was enclosed in 1886 and developed as agricultural land, and around the time of World War II supported a cricket ground! Plans to regenerate the saltmarsh started in 1995, and today it provides suitable habitats for a wide range of flora and fauna, with large numbers of migrant waders; look out for flocks of curlews in winter, and deep red samphire beds in autumn.

the ride

1 Return to the lane, turn right and descend into Clearbrook and continue past **The Skylark Inn** for about 500yds (457m). Turn right opposite the village hall on a track. After 100yds (91m) turn right up a steep, narrow path; at the top by the **pylon** bear left downhill (cyclists should dismount). This turns sharp left, then right through a gate onto the rough, gritty, old railway line. Follow this for about 0.5 mile (0.8km) to **Goodameavy**, where tarmac takes over. (Note: to avoid this initial rough section turn left at the fork by the parking area, signed 'Goodameavy', and cycle steeply downhill to join the railway.)

2 Soon after Goodameavy the track passes through **Shaugh Tunnel** (note: there are lights, but these are turned off between dusk and dawn – there's a colony of roosting bats in the tunnel), and then under an aqueduct. Pass Shaugh Bridge Halt and cross **Ham Green viaduct**; look back left and you'll catch sight of the Dewerstone Rock above the wooded Plym Valley just above its junction with the River Meavy.

3 At **Ham Bridge** the route meets a lane; turn right uphill towards **Bickleigh**. At the T-junction turn left and proceed very steeply downhill (young children should dismount). Turn right on a narrow wooded path back onto the railway line and continue through deciduous woodland. Pass over Bickleigh viaduct and into the National Trust's **Plym Bridge Woods**. Continue over Cann viaduct – look over the left side to see the remains of Rumple wheelpit by the river below, and the face of **Cann Quarry** beyond.

4 At Plym Bridge follow signs sharp left to leave the track. For a picnic by the river, turn left under the railway towards the 18th-century bridge; the meadow is on the right (leave your bikes on the lane). For **Saltram House** – created in the 18th century with 500 acres (202ha) of parkland – cross the car park entrance and turn right on a level woodland track. Cycle towards Plymouth (note that Plymouth is one end of the Devon Coast to Coast route, which runs for 102 miles/163km to Ilfracombe – watch out for serious and speedy cyclists!) to emerge by **Coypool Park-and-Ride** on the right.

5 Cross the road at the T-junction and follow the narrow path ahead (barrier); cross the next road and take the rough track opposite. Just past the **playing field gates** (right) bear right on a narrow path to emerge under the A38. Bear diagonally right to find a railed tarmac path uphill left. Follow that up and down, then along the edge of the Plym Estuary until you reach the National Trust's **Saltram Estate**.

6 At the edge of parkland keep right, and follow the estuary to **Point Cottage**. Turn left inland on an estate lane to cross the parking area, with the house and **shop** left. At the signpost bear left, signed **'Riverside walk and bird hide'** and cycle carefully downhill, avoiding pedestrians, keeping straight on where the tarmac way bears left towards offices. Re-enter the **parkland** and keep ahead to rejoin the outward route.

3h00 – **13.5 MILES** – **21.7 KM** – **LEVEL 123**

SHORTER ALTERNATIVE ROUTE

2h15 – **10.5 MILES** – **16.9 KM** – **LEVEL 123**

MAP: OS Explorer OL20 South Devon

START/FINISH: Clearbook parking area above village, grid ref SX518650

TRAILS/TRACKS: mix of bumpy and well-surfaced track

LANDSCAPE: wooded valley, townscape, estuary and parkland on extension

PUBLIC TOILETS: Coypool (Point **5**)

TOURIST INFORMATION: Plymouth, tel 01752 304849

CYCLE HIRE: Tavistock Cycles, Tavistock, tel 01822 617630

THE PUB: The Skylark Inn, Clearbrook

! First 0.75 mile (1.2km) rough and bumpy (alternative lane access given), steep hills at Bickleigh and busy roads on extension

Getting to the start

Clearbrook lies on Dartmoor's western edge, clearly signposted off the A386 Tavistock to Plymouth road, 2.5 miles (4km) south of Yelverton. Follow the lane across the down and park at the furthest parking area on the right where the road forks.

Why do this cycle ride?

This ride – particularly if the extension to Saltram House is included – covers an impressive range of landscapes: moorland, woodland, river estuary and parkland. The views at both the northern (Dartmoor) and southern (Plym Estuary) ends are impressive, and the outskirts of Plymouth, for Saltram House, passed quickly.

Researched and written by: Sue Viccars

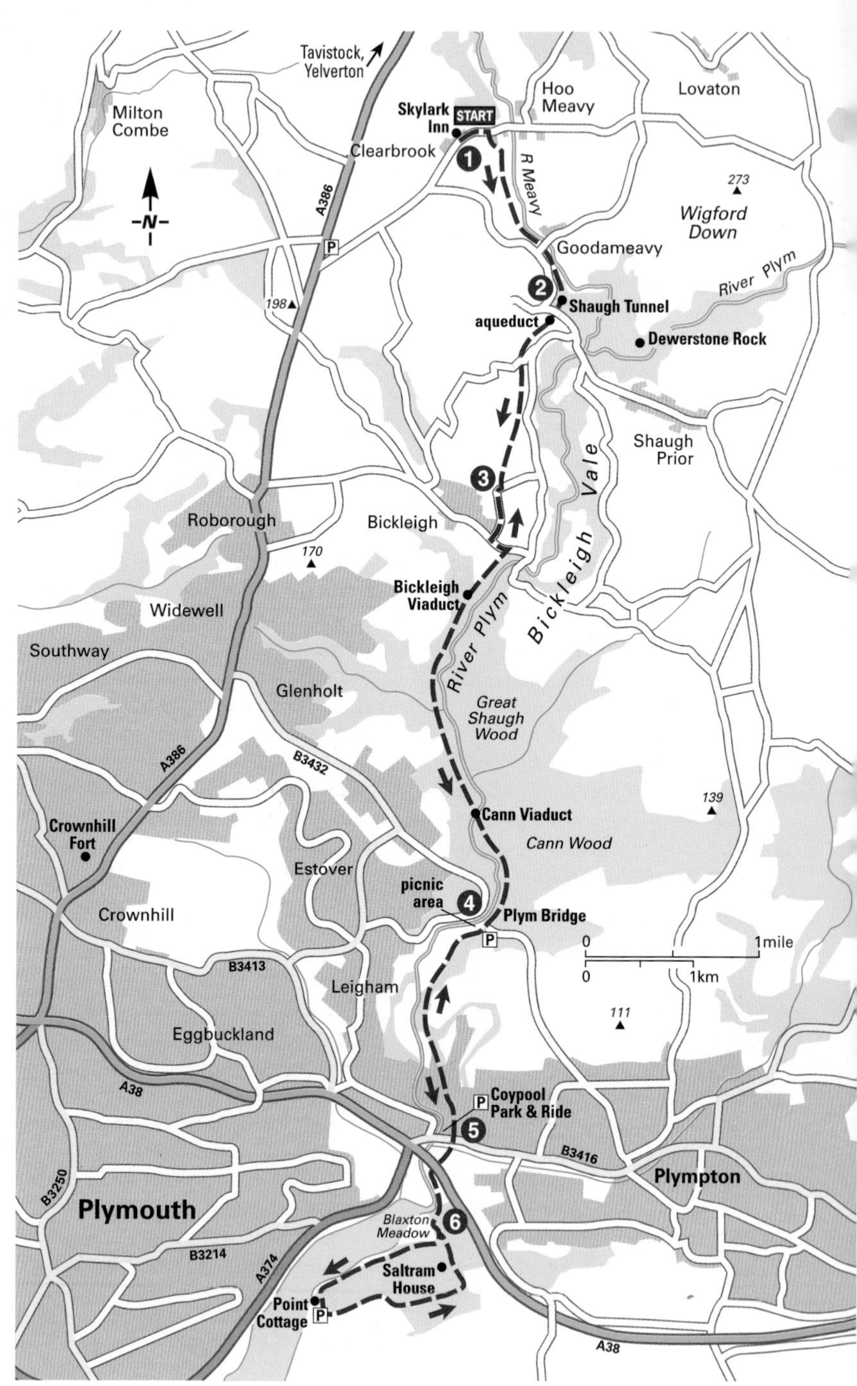
Tavistock, Yelverton
Milton Combe
Skylark Inn
START
Hoo Meavy
Lovaton
Clearbrook
R Meavy
273
Wigford Down
A386
Goodameavy
River Plym
198
Shaugh Tunnel
aqueduct
Dewerstone Rock
Shaugh Prior
Bickleigh Vale
Roborough
Bickleigh
170
Bickleigh Viaduct
Widewell
River Plym
Southway
Glenholt
Great Shaugh Wood
A386
B3432
139
Cann Viaduct
Cann Wood
Crownhill Fort
Estover
picnic area
Plym Bridge
Crownhill
0 1mile
0 1km
B3413
Leigham
111
Eggbuckland
A38
Coypool Park & Ride
B3416
Plympton
B3250
Plymouth
Blaxton Meadow
B3214
A374
Saltram House
Point Cottage
A38

The Skylark Inn

Although only minutes from Plymouth, you will find the Skylark tucked away in a pretty row of cottages in a sleepy village on the southern flanks of Dartmoor. It's a welcoming two-room pub; the beamed main bar is simply furnished and boasts a big fireplace with wood-burning stove. Although very much a lively local the pub also bustles with passing walkers and cyclists exploring the National Park. There's a large back garden for summer alfresco eating and drinking.

Food

Good wholesome food is served from an extensive menu that features filled baguettes, battered cod with chips, pasta meals, short-crust pastry pies and speciality salads such as Crayfish and Greek. Sunday roast lunches.

about the pub

The Skylark Inn
Clearbrook, Yelverton
Devon PL20 6JD
Tel 01822 853258
www.theskylarkinn.co.uk

DIRECTIONS: see Getting to the start; descend into Clearbrook and the Skylark Inn is on the left

PARKING: 16

OPEN: daily; all day Saturday and Sunday

FOOD: lunchtime and evening

BREWERY/COMPANY: Unique Inns

REAL ALE: Courage Best, 6X and Otterhead

Family facilities

Children are welcome in the rear family room (no under 14s in the bar). There's a children's menu and an adventure play area in the garden.

Alternative refreshment stops

There is a licensed café at Saltram House.

☛ Where to go from here

At Buckland Monachorum you'll find Buckland Abbey, formerly a 13th-century Cistercian Abbey, which was sold to Sir Francis Drake in 1581. He lived here until his death in 1596. Restored buildings house a fascinating exhibition about the abbey's history, including Drake's drum (www.nationaltrust.org.uk). At the National Marine Aquarium in Plymouth, Britain's biggest aquarium, you can see 15 species of shark and ray, walk through an underwater tunnel and enter the Twilight Zone (www.national-aquarium.co.uk). Discover Plymouth's past and much more at the Plymouth Dome, a high-tech visitor centre with audio-visual commentaries and observation galleries (www.plymouthdome.gov.uk). If you visit Saltram House by bike, your entry fee is refunded (www.nationaltrust.org.uk).

12

Along the Dart Valley Trail

Cycle through woods and parkland above the tranquil River Dart south of the historic town of Totnes.

The Dart Valley Trail

Totnes and Ashprington

The River Dart at Totnes – today a focus for tourists and pleasure craft – has always played an important part in the fortunes of the town. At the lowest crossing point of the river, the first stone bridge was built in the early 13th century. By Tudor times Totnes was Devon's second most important port, heavily involved in the woollen industry, and also exporting tin and granite from Dartmoor's mines. Even back in the 10th century there was a Saxon burgh here; later the Normans made their mark by building the motte-and-bailey castle that dominates the town even today. From the motte you can clearly see the structure of the town, the original parts of which were walled in the 12th century. Totnes still has many fine 15th- and 16th-century buildings.

When you cycle downhill into Ashprington you feel as if you've entered something of a time warp. This pretty village, nestling in the folds of the hills, was originally part of the Sharpham Estate, though many of the buildings were sold off in 1940. Despite this most retain the characteristic lattice

12

2h00 | 7 MILES | 11.3 KM | LEVEL 123

windows and bargeboarded gables, made by the estate carpenter, and the village has a pleasing uniformity.

the ride

1 From the car park follow the road back towards Totnes. Turn left onto Seymour Road, then left over **Totnes Bridge** (built to replace a smaller one in 1838, and a toll bridge until 1881) – the lowest crossing point of the Dart – to reach the roundabout at the bottom of Fore Street. Turn left along **The Plains**, at one time an area of tidal marsh; the old riverside warehouses have now been converted into stylish accommodation. Keep ahead along New Walk to reach the **Steam Packet Inn** on the left.

2 As the road bends sharp left turn right up narrow tarmac **Moat Hill**. After about 20yds (18m) turn left as signed 'Ashprington' on a gritty, fenced track, gently uphill.

3 At the end bear right then left onto the old driveway to **Sharpham House**, initially walled. Pass out into the open briefly – look back for good views over the river at Totnes – then back into woodland. Continue uphill to cross a cattle grid in woodland. There follows a lovely downhill run through parkland, with fantastic views ahead left over reedbeds fringing the river. The ride runs uphill into woodland again and passes into the **Sharpham Estate** via a gate. Continue through two more gates and back into parkland – watch out for cowpats beneath your wheels and cows in front of you! A long downhill run, with **Linhay Plantation** right, leads towards the river. Pass through a gate on a track to reach a signpost.

MAP: OS Explorer OL20 South Devon
START/FINISH: Steamer Quay (or Longmarsh) car park, grid ref: SX809596
TRAILS/TRACKS: country house drive, rough woodland path, tarmac lane
LANDSCAPE: river valley, parkland, rolling woods and farmland
PUBLIC TOILETS: Steamer Quay, Totnes
TOURIST INFORMATION: Totnes, tel 01803 863168
CYCLE HIRE: B R Trott Cycle Hire, Warland Garage, Totnes, tel 01803 862493
THE PUB: The Durant Arms, Ashprington
! Steep ascent/descent through woodland near Ashprington: cyclists should dismount

Getting to the start

Totnes lies on the A385 between the A38 and Torbay. Follow signs for the Steamer Quay from the bottom of Fore Street. If Steamer Quay is full, keep ahead to Longmarsh overflow car park.

Why do this cycle ride?

The ideal escape route from the hustle and bustle of Totnes – which can get very busy in holiday times – to the peaceful, beautiful valley of the River Dart. The ride undulates through parkland and meadows of the Sharpham Estate, overlooking the meandering Dart, before a tough climb through woodland. The delightful village of Ashprington, and The Durant Arms provide a great – and welcome! – focus.

Researched and written by: Sue Viccars

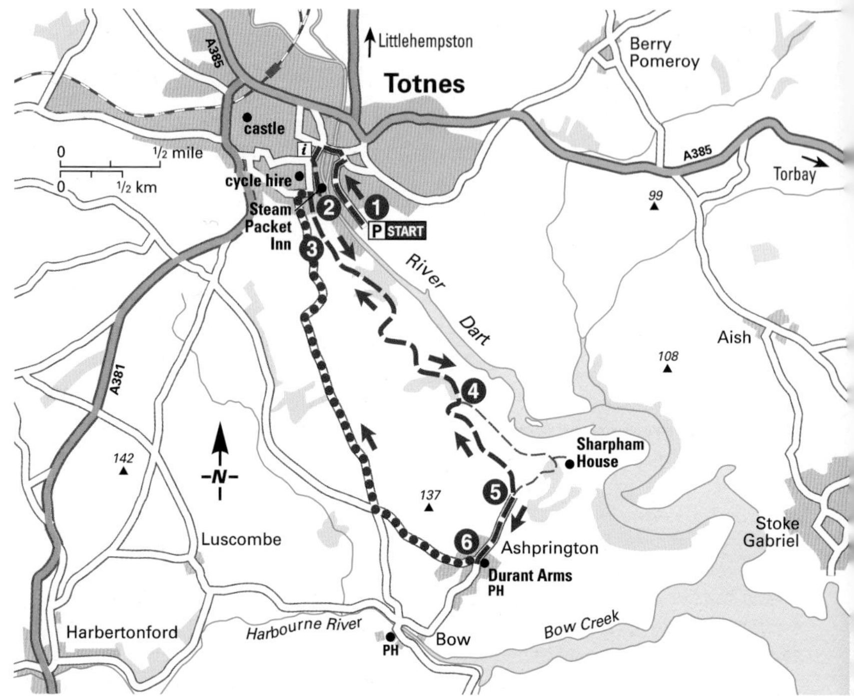

4 Turn right along a narrow gritty track that runs uphill away from the river. Follow this as it bears left with the hedge and continues uphill. Pass over a **cattle grid**, at which point cyclists are asked to dismount. Continue up the rough, rooty track – Leafy Lane – through **Lower Gribble Plantation** – it's quite a slog. Pass through a staggered barrier; the track levels off and reaches a lane, with the entrance to **Sharpham House** left. Sharpham House was built in the late 18th century – replacing an Elizabethan building – for Captain Philemon Pownall of HMS *Favourite*, funded by prize money from the capture of a Spanish treasure ship. His grandson later lost Sharpham when he gambled away the family fortune. Situated on the warm south-facing slopes above the Dart, the estate now hosts a working vineyard and cheese dairy, and has a shop and café – definitely worth a visit.

5 Turn right along the narrow and quiet lane for 0.5 mile (800m). A pleasant downhill run ends in the centre of Ashprington. **The Durant Arms** – an inn since 1725 and renamed in honour of the Durant family of Sharpham – will be found on the left.

6 To return to Totnes, it would be possible to follow a different route along the undulating country lanes. Turn right at the **war memorial** in Ashprington and follow the lane to Ashprington Cross. Turn right and follow that lane all the way back to meet **Moat Hill**; turn right for New Walk. However, Devon lanes are usually narrow and twisty, with high hedges and poor visibility; it's far safer to return by the outward route (which has lovely views north towards Dartmoor).

The Durant Arms

Off the tourist trail in the popular South Hams and situated in the heart of a sleepy village, this neat and tidy, cream-painted 18th-century pub has developed a local clientele, who favour the honest home-cooked food that can be enjoyed here. A flagged entrance hall leads into the beamed, open-plan bar, with a popular window seat overlooking the village street, and into the spick-and-span dining rooms, adorned with oils and watercolours by local artists. A small terraced garden with hardwood furniture and a water feature makes a pleasant alternative to the bar in warm weather.

Food

Very good food using fresh local produce ranges from hearty steak and kidney pie and ham, egg and chips to sirloin steak and a blackboard listing the day's fresh fish, where you may find halibut, lemon sole, and scallops and tiger prawns in cream and white wine sauce. Sandwiches are available at lunchtime.

Family facilities

There's a separate children's area away from the bar and children are welcome inside the pub provided they are eating. A flexible menu and half-portions of some main menu dishes are available, as is one high chair. No children overnight.

about the pub

The Durant Arms
Ashprington, Totnes
Devon TQ9 7UP
Tel 01803 732240
www.thedurantarms.com

DIRECTIONS: village is signposted off the A381 south of Totnes; pub in the square

PARKING: 7 (+ street parking)

OPEN: daily

FOOD: daily

BREWERY/COMPANY: free house

REAL ALE: St Austell Tribute and Dartmoor Best

ROOMS: 8 en suite

Alternative refreshment stops

There's a good choice of cafés and pubs, including the Steam Packet Inn in Totnes, and there's a café at Sharpham Vineyard.

☛ Where to go from here

Enjoy a steam train trip through the lovely, unspoilt scenery of the wooded Dart Valley from Totnes to Buckfastleigh on the South Devon Railway (www.southdevonrailway.org). Take a cruise along the River Dart to Dartmouth (www.riverlink.co.uk), explore the streets of Totnes and visit the town's castle, one of the best surviving examples of a Norman motte-and-bailey castle (www.english-heritage.org.uk). Attractions near Newton Abbot include the Devon Bird of Prey Centre (www.devonbirdofprey.co.uk), and the Hedgehog Hospital and British Wildlife Garden Centre (www.hedgehog.org.uk), while Torquay offers a wealth of things to see and do, including Babbacombe Model Village (www.babbacombemodelvillage.co.uk), Kent's Cavern (www.kent-cavern.co.uk), and Living Coasts which explores coastlines around the world without leaving Torquay (www.livingcoasts.org.uk).

Exeter Ship Canal

Follow the banks of the historic Exeter Ship Canal from the heart of the city to the Turf Lock, where the canal rejoins the Exe estuary.

Exeter

Quite apart from the old quayside, there's much to explore in Exeter itself. There has been a settlement here, at the lowest crossing point of the Exe, since before the Romans established Isca Dumnoniorum (named after the local tribe) in AD 50. The settlement marked the western limit of Roman occupation of the south-west, and about two thirds of the Roman city walls are still visible today. In the 1970s the magnificent Roman bathhouse was excavated, and now lies protected beneath paving slabs outside the West Front of the Norman Cathedral Church of St Peter. Largely built of Beer stone, quarried from the cliffs of east Devon, the cathedral's intricately carved West Front is stunning. The twin towers survived an extensive rebuild from 1270 to 1360.

Exeter has a wealth of medieval churches, and the Cathedral Close has examples of Tudor and Stuart architecture, which miraculously escaped bomb damage in May 1942. The 16th-century Ship Inn in St Martin's Lane is reputed to have been visited by Sir Francis Drake, and black-and-white timbered Mol's Coffee House on the corner of The Close dates from that time.

Cycling on the Exe Valley Way, part of the Exeter Ship Canal

the ride

1 From Saddles & Paddles cross the quay to the riverside. Turn right and cycle upstream to **Cricklepit Bridge** (built in 1905); turn right over the bridge, and right again on the other side. Cycle along the broad **riverside walkway**, passing Bar Venezia and Roger's Tearoom on the right. Keep ahead to cycle between the river on the left and canal basin (originally called The New Cut) on the right, built in 1830 to extend ship accommodation at the Exeter end of the canal. Pass **Trew's Weir**, and the **Port Royal** on the opposite bank, to reach the canal (Welcome Inn ahead right).

Storm clouds over the canal basin

13

2h15 · 12 MILES · 19.3 KM · LEVEL 1 2 3

2 Turn left over the canal; turn right along the tarmac way between the canal and the flood prevention 'trough'. Where the path forks, keep left. Look for yellow flag iris and purple loosestrife below left. Pass **playing fields** on the right, bearing right at the end to reach the canal by a small car park (right).

3 Do not cross the canal; turn left on a **tarmac cycle track** that parallels the canal. The track bears away from the canal to pass to the left of the Double Locks pub, built in 1702. Continue on to a fork just before the A379, passing the **Double Locks Wetlands** on the left, a managed area of reedbeds which is a haven for wildflowers, dragonflies, birds and insects.

4 Take the right fork; cross the A379 at the **traffic lights** (note the swing bridge over the canal). On the other side, the track becomes (initially) narrower and rougher. Pass a small parking area (right), then cycle under the M5; from now on you're out in peaceful countryside. The Exe Estuary silted up during the 14th century, and the canal – renowned as being the earliest working ship canal in England – was started around 1564, linking Exeter to Trenchard's Sluice (which entered the river by the M5 viaduct). The canal was extended to Topsham (a port since Roman times, seen across the canal and river to the left) in 1676. In the early 19th century – under the engineer James Green – it reached the Turf Lock. Its fortunes deteriorated after Brunel's railway reached Exeter in 1844, and then Exmouth (on the east side of the estuary) in 1861.

MAP: OS Explorer 114 Exeter & the Exe Valley and 110 Torquay & Dawlish

START/FINISH: The Quay, Exeter, grid ref: SX920920

TRAILS/TRACKS: well-surfaced path

LANDSCAPE: rural townscape, canal and estuary, marsh

PUBLIC TOILETS: at the start

TOURIST INFORMATION: Exeter, tel 01392 265700

CYCLE HIRE: Saddles and Paddles, The Quay, Exeter, tel 01392 424241

THE PUB: The Turf Hotel, Exminster

! Busy crossing of A379 (but traffic lights for walkers/cyclists)

Getting to the start

Exeter Quay lies on the north side of the River Exe in the old West Quarter. Follow brown tourist signs (with an anchor logo) for the quayside. There is no parking on the quay. Park in the Cathedral and Quay car park, just above The Quay.

Why do this cycle ride?

Exeter has an impressive maritime heritage, and this ride starts and finishes at the very hub: the old quayside. The route runs through a lovely stretch of 'inner city' countryside before striking south along the canal through nature reserves and marshes to reach the Turf Hotel, situated on the Exe estuary.

Researched and written by: Sue Viccars

13

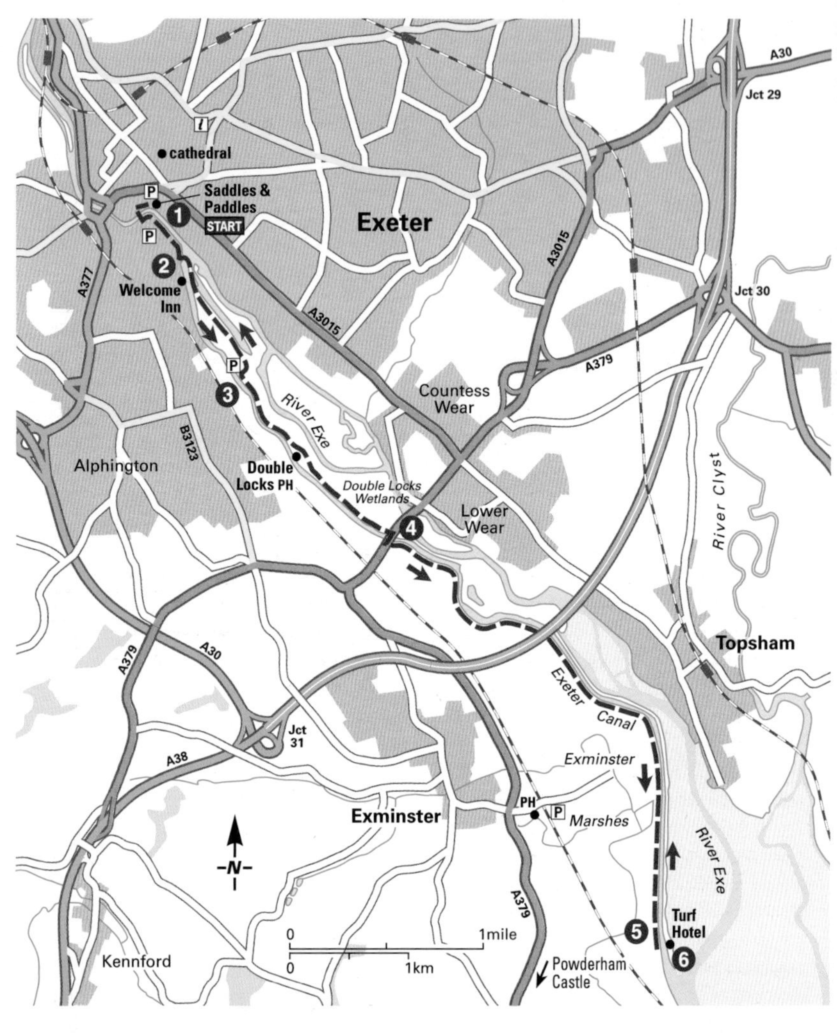

5 Arrive at the basin of the **Turf Lock** (constructed in 1827), where the canal reaches the Exe Estuary and you have lovely views ahead towards the sea. The building housing The Turf Hotel was thought to have been built at around the same time, and it was probably used to accommodate visiting boat crews. Horse-drawn barges then transported goods up the canal to Exeter.

6 Cycle back to **Exeter**. Exminster Marshes (this side) and Bowling Green marshes (on the other side of the estuary) are RSPB reserves, so keep an eye out for birdlife. Spring brings lapwing and redshank; through autumn and winter thousands of curlew, widgeon, teal, golden plover and dunlin, for example, come here to feed and roost. It's also important for migrant birds, including elegant avocets.

The Turf Hotel

Built around 1830, and remotely situated at the end of Exeter Canal with tranquil views across the Exe estuary and out to sea, the Turf is one of the few pubs in the country that cannot be reached by car. Arrive by boat, by ferry from Starcross, Topsham or Exeter, by bicycle, or after a 20-minute walk beside the canal. It's worth the effort for the views and the summer cook-your-own barbecue in the huge garden. If the weather is inclement, the simply decorated bar is equally appealing, with its bare board floor, rustic panelled walls, wood-burning stove, eclectic mix of wooden tables and chairs, and bay window-seats with views across the bird-rich mudflats. First-rate Otter beers on hand-pump and local farm cider.

Food

At lunch tuck into sandwiches, filled jacket potatoes, pizzas, chicken and Brie ciabatta and home-made chilli with taco chips. Evening additions include Thai chicken curry, sirloin steak and blackboard specials like fresh mussels or Exe salmon.

Family facilities

Children are welcome everywhere and they will love playing in the old boat in the garden.

about the pub

The Turf Hotel
Turf Locks, Exminster
Exeter, Devon EX6 8EE
Tel 01392 833128
www.turfpub.net

DIRECTIONS: the pub cannot be reached by car; nearest parking 0.75 mile (1.2km) up the canal and accessed from the A379 Dawlish road, turning left at the mini-roundabout at the end of the Exminster by-pass

PARKING: none – see above

OPEN: daily; all day June to August; Saturday and Sunday April, May and September; weekends only until 6pm October and March; closed November to February

FOOD: no food Sunday evenings

BREWERY/COMPANY: free house

REAL ALE: Otter Ale, Ferryman's Ale and Yellow Hammer

Alternative refreshment stops

The Double Locks pub beside the canal on your route out of Exeter. There are plenty of pubs, cafés and restaurants in Exeter.

☛ Where to go from here

Take a cruise on the Exeter Canal (www.exetercruises.com) or spend some time exploring the city of Exeter, notably St Nicholas Priory, founded in 1087 and featuring a Norman undercroft, a Tudor room and 15th-century kitchen. Enjoy a guided tour of Exeter's most unusual medieval attraction, the atmospheric network of underground passages, built in the 13th century to bring water into the city (www.exeter.gov.uk). Set in beautiful rose gardens and a deer park beside the River Exe, Powderham Castle is the ancestral home of the Earls of Devon.

14

Along the Grand Western Canal to Tiverton

A wonderfully peaceful ride along the banks of the old Grand Western Canal through the GWC Country Park and the beautiful countryside of mid Devon.

Flora & fauna

Disused canals in rural areas provide ideal wildlife habitats, and when you cycle along the Grand Western Canal you certainly feel outnumbered by members of the bird and animal kingdom. This is an ideal site for the water vole – Britain's largest vole, also known as the water rat – whose numbers have fallen drastically in recent years due to a reduction in suitable habitats. There are coots, moorhens and mallards on the water, and robins, starlings, chaffinches and blackbirds around the many picnic spots along the way. You may spot a heron or a kingfisher by the water.

It's a wonderful place for wildflowers, too: parts of this beautiful reed-fringed canal are carpeted with expanses of white water lilies, harvested until the mid 1960s from a horse-drawn boat. They were laid out at Sampford Peverell wharf, packed and sent around the country to be used in funeral wreaths. You should also see cuckooflower, meadowsweet and yellow loosestrife (uncommon elsewhere in Devon), arrowhead and yellow flag iris rooted in the water's edge, dragonflies, damselflies and butterflies.

the ride

1 From the back of the car park, pass the **tennis court** (left), bear left round a gate and uphill to the towpath (don't go too fast or you might overshoot!). Construction of the canal began in 1810, part of a grand scheme to link the English and Bristol Channels via Exeter and Bristol, but only the Tiverton and Taunton stretch was

Below and right: Canal boats towed along the Grand Western Canal by draught horse

14

2h15 | 11 MILES | 17.7 KM | LEVEL 123

MAP: OS Explorer 128 Taunton & Blackdown Hills and 114 Exeter & the Exe Valley

START/FINISH: Sampford Peverell, grid ref: ST030142

TRAILS/TRACKS: good canalside path, some stretches grassy, most gritty

LANDSCAPE: canal towpath, farmland, rural townscape

PUBLIC TOILETS: at start and at Tiverton Canal Basin (Point **6**)

TOURIST INFORMATION: Tiverton, tel 01884 255827

CYCLE HIRE: Abbotshood Cycle Hire, Halberton, tel 01884 820728

THE PUB: Globe Inn, Sampford Peverell

! Path narrows under bridges - cyclists advised to dismount

Getting to the start

Sampford Peverell lies west of M5 junction 27 (Tiverton Parkway). From the M5 follow the A361 Tiverton road; at the first exit (0.5 mile/800m) leave the A361, bear left at the roundabout, and continue into the village. The public car park is signed to the right.

Why do this cycle ride?

The vast majority of visitors to Devon head straight for the coast or moors, and many don't think about exploring the county's heartland. This quiet route along the towpath of the old Grand Western Canal takes you right through the rolling mid-Devon farmland to the centre of Tiverton.

Researched and written by: Sue Viccars

completed. This section – Lowdwells to Tiverton – was completed in 1814. Competition from the railways eventually forced the closure of the canal, although this section of water was used to transport limestone from quarries around Westleigh to Tiverton until as late as 1924.

2 Turn left along the tow path, passing the **Globe Inn**. Pass under **Sampford Peverell bridge** (best to dismount) and continue along a short stretch of quiet lane. Where that bears left, keep ahead along the canalside and you're immediately out in the countryside, with good views of the wooded **Blackdown Hills** to the left – you feel as if you're miles from anywhere. Pass under **Battens Bridge**, then **Rock Bridge**. The next bridge is made of metal. These bridges– look out for them along the cycle route – were originally wooden swing bridges, enabling the passage of barges and linking farmers' land where it was split up by the canal.

14

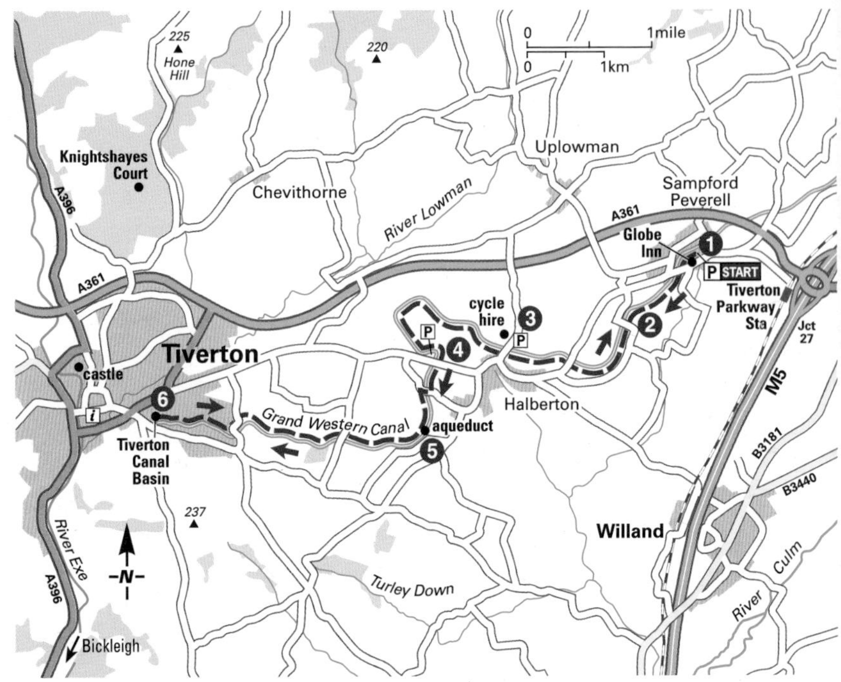

3 Continue along an embanked stretch to pass under Greenway Bridge (car park) and then **Sellake Bridge**. Note how the canal takes a wide sweep (270°) to the left; this is known as the Swan's Neck, and was necessary to avoid the village of Halberton.

4 Next stop is **Tiverton Road Bridge** (car park and picnic area), where you may see canoes and kayaks. There was once a stone-crushing yard here; the journey from a quarry 8 miles (12.9km) away at Whipcott took 2.5 hours, with two horses pulling three 8–10 ton barges. Note milestone III on the left; it's only 3 miles (4.8km) to the basin at Tiverton. Keep on to **Crownhill Bridge**, once known as 'Change Path'. Horses had to change to the right bank here; you do the same by crossing the bridge and turning left.

5 Cross the brick **aqueduct** of the Bristol and Exeter Railway line, built in 1847. This – the Tiverton branch – closed to passenger traffic in 1964. Three more bridges bring you to neat hedges and bungalows marking the edge of Tiverton. Tidcombe Bridge (look out for milestone I) marks another loop, made necessary by the Bishop of Exeter's refusal to allow the canal within 100yds (91m) of his home (Tidcombe Hall) near by.

6 **Tiverton Canal Basin**, built in 1842, makes an excellent focus for this ride. Refreshments are available at the thatched 16th-century Canal Tearooms, below the basin to the right, or from the floating Barge Canal shop. Look out too for the old limekilns to the right; limestone was burnt here until the late 19th century to produce fertiliser. Farmers are said to have travelled up to 30 miles (nearly 50km) – each way! – by horse and cart to collect it. To return to **Sampford Peverell**, simply follow the canal towpath back the way you came.

Globe Inn

(14)

Handily placed just a mile from the M5 (J27) and beside the Grand Western Canal in a peaceful village, the Globe draws passing travellers and visiting walkers and fishermen exploring the delights of the canal. Beyond the stone and timber façade there's a spacious locals' bar with bare boards, wood-panelled walls and a stone fireplace with a wood-burning stove. The adjoining lounge bar and dining area is carpeted with stone walls and a beamed ceiling. There's also a pretty, flower-decked rear patio with smart tables and chairs and heaters for cool evenings.

about the pub

Globe Inn
16 Lower Town, Sampford Peverell
Tiverton, Devon EX16 7BJ
Tel 01884 821214
www.globe-inn.com

DIRECTIONS: see Getting to the start
PARKING: 60
OPEN: daily; all day
FOOD: daily; all day in summer
BREWERY/COMPANY: Enterprise Inns
REAL ALE: Otter Bright, Otter Bitter and Otter Head
ROOMS: 6 en suite

Food

A traditional pub menu takes in a wide range of filled baps and salad platters, standard favourites like haddock and chips, light meals like goat's cheese and tomato tart, and specials like steak, kidney and ale pie and mixed grill. Roast carvery lunches on Sunday.

Family facilities

Children are allowed throughout the pub; there's a children's menu and an excellent play area in the garden.

Alternative refreshment stops

Plenty of choice in Tiverton.

☛ Where to go from here

In Tiverton make time to see the castle, view the 15 galleries at the interesting Museum of Mid Devon Life (www.tivertonmuseum.org.uk), and the town's famous Pannier Market. Cross the M5 to Uffculme to view the Coldharbour Mill Working Wool Museum, which has been producing textiles since 1790. There are machine demonstrations, a water wheel and steam engines (www.coldharbourmill.org.uk). Visit Bickleigh Castle, a fortified manor house that boasts a fascinating history. The restored gatehouse, the ancient chapel and the cob and thatch farmhouse can all be visited (www.bickleighcastle.com).

15 Exmouth to Knowle

Explore the old Exmouth to Budleigh Salterton railway line with the chance of a stop at the pub in Knowle.

The Jurassic coast

No visit to this part of Devon would be complete without a visit to the coast, so accomplish that before starting this cycle ride. Go down to Exmouth's sea front and have a drink at The Grove, which has fabulous views across Exmouth's 2 mile (3.2km) long sandy beach both out to sea and across the Exe estuary to the sandspit and nature reserve at Dawlish Warren.

The coastline from Exmouth all the way to Old Harry Rocks on the Isle of Purbeck in Dorset – 95 miles (155km) away – was awarded World Heritage Site status in 2001, the first in England. It's hard to imagine, but the red rocks of this part of east Devon date back around 200 to 250 million years, the Triassic period, when hot desert conditions prevailed. The red colouring comes from the weathering of iron minerals (similar to the Namib Desert in Africa today). The Geoneedle on the red cliffs at Orcombe Point, just east of Exmouth, marks the inauguration of the World Heritage Site. You can take a boat trip along the coast from Exmouth past Budleigh Salterton's famous pebble beds, deposited by one of the huge rivers that flowed through the desert over 200 million years ago. Today the beds are piled up to form a large and attractive part of the beach.

the ride

1 From the car park cycle back downhill to the entrance to the park. Turn left on the road and cycle up **Marpool Hill** for about 200yds (183m). Turn left where signed on the cycleway/path (note that cyclists should keep on the left). Follow this tarmac way – watch out for pedestrians – along the top of the park, then between houses, to meet a road.

One of the information boards found on the designated cycle trail

2 Turn right on the pavement up to the traffic lights. Dismount to cross the B3178; turn left, then right after 20yds (18m). Follow this narrow winding tarmac way between fences – take care – to reach another road at **Littleham Cross** (Exmoor Motor Spares, 20yds/18m, left, sells cycle repair kits etc). Cross the road and cycle along Jarvis Close. Keep ahead on a tarmac way, which bears left downhill, then right to reach **Littleham Road**.

3 Cross over. You can push your bike straight ahead on a narrow way between bungalows, or turn right down the road for 100yds (91m), then left into **Bidmead Close**. After 20yds (18m) bear right uphill on a tarmac path – John Hudson Close – to rejoin the old **railway line**.

4 Follow the track under a bridge (Capel Lane – access to the route, and also to the Clinton Arms in Littleham) and on into open countryside. Pass a picnic table on the right with views towards **Dawlish Warren**, and over the 15th-century tower of Littleham's Church of St Margaret and St Andrew, where Lady Nelson is buried. The track becomes gritty and runs pleasantly through farmland, then through **Knowle Hill plantations** (access to Castle Lane). When the line opened in 1903 it was said that it ran through 'beautiful hills and beautiful meadows, with bright colours of earth and field and woodland and gay flowers beside the line'. Sadly it never realised its full potential, and fell to Beeching's axe; the last train ran on 4 March 1967. The cycle route was opened in 1998, and has become a haven for wildlife and flowers.

2h00 – 11 MILES – 17.6 KM – LEVEL 123

SHORTER ALTERNATIVE ROUTE

1h45 – 10 MILES – 16 KM – LEVEL 123

MAP: OS Explorer 115 Exmouth & Sidmouth

START/FINISH: Phear Park, Exmouth, grid ref: SY008815

TRAILS/TRACKS: mainly well-surfaced track, short stretches on broad pavements

LANDSCAPE: townscape, woodland and farmland

PUBLIC TOILETS: Phear Park, and just off the route at Littleham Cross (Point **2**)

TOURIST INFORMATION: Exmouth, tel 01395 222299

THE PUB: The Grove, Exmouth

! Busy B3178 to pub at Knowle (pavement)

Getting to the start

Exmouth lies east of the mouth of the Exe on the south Devon coast. From the A376 turn left at traffic lights into Gipsy Lane. At the roundabout turn right, then left into Phear Park. From the B3178 Salterton Road turn right. Descend Marpool Hill, bear right at the roundabout, and right into Phear Park.

Why do this cycle ride?

The route follows part of 'The Buzzard', an 80-mile (129km) circular ride through east Devon. It's an easy, quiet ride, mainly along the old Exmouth to Budleigh railway line. There's an optional 1 mile (1.6km) extension at the end for refreshments at the child-friendly Dog and Donkey in Knowle.

Researched and written by: Sue Viccars

15

5 At this point pass under another bridge on the top of **Knowle Hill** – the deep cutting here was mainly dug out by hand, with the help of two 'steam navvies' (early steam-driven shovels) – then enjoy a long gentle downhill run that passes under a row of shady beech trees. Leave the track on a tarmac way that bears right uphill to reach **Bear Lane**, from where there is a glimpse ahead of the wooded top of **High Peak** (515ft/157m) on the coast, site of an important Iron Age fort.

6 For a break at the pub, turn right down Bear Lane to the B3178. Turn right downhill (take care – fortunately there is a pavement) to find the Dog and Donkey at the bottom of the hill on the left. To return to **Exmouth**, retrace the route. It is possible to cycle on to **Budleigh Salterton** – named after salt pans that used to be sited at the mouth of the River Otter, the estuary of which is now a nature reserve – but the roads tend to be busy and so this is not recommended for families.

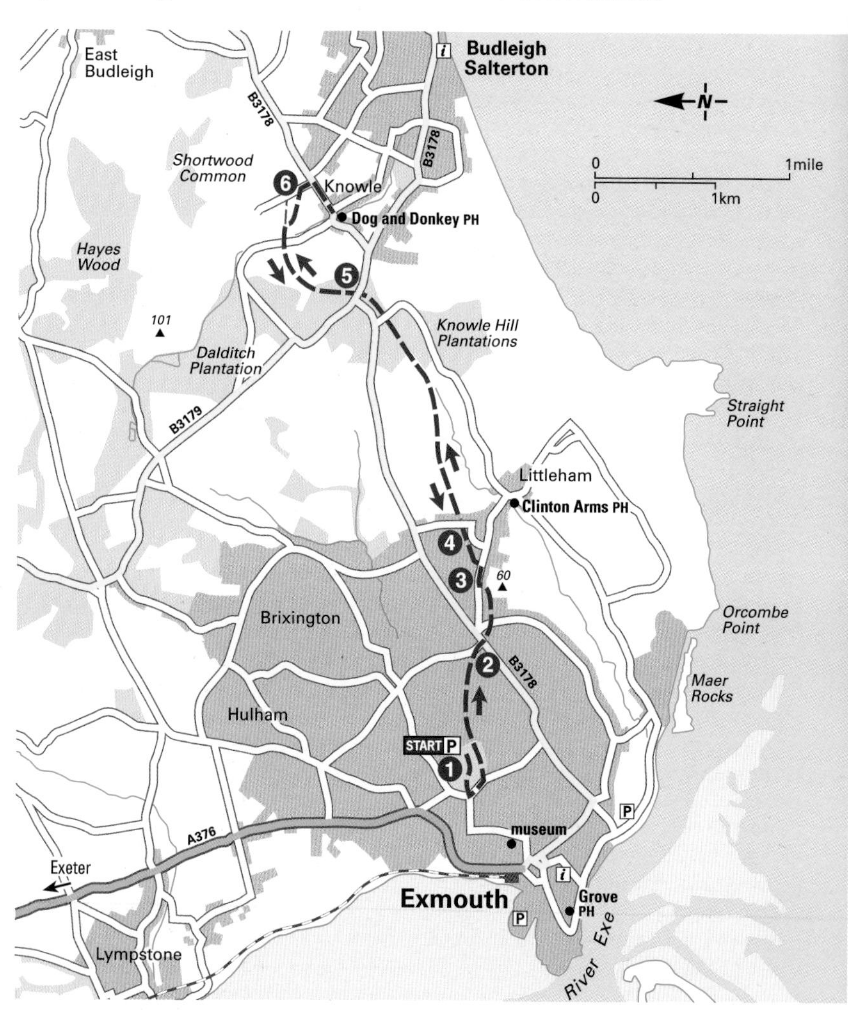

The Grove

A smartly refurbished Young's pub set back from the beach, with a first-floor dining room and balcony enjoying spectacular views across the mouth of the River Exe and along the coast to Torbay. The sheltered rear garden is a super spot for rest and refreshment after time spent on the bike or beach. Inside, the roomy panelled bars are comfortably furnished and feature open fires, well-kept beers, decent wines by the glass, and local prints on the walls.

Food

A menu listing traditional British dishes highlights steak and Young's ale pie, Cumberland sausages and mash, fish pie, beer battered fish and chips, and ham, egg and chips. Lighter meals include ploughman's lunches, various paninis and Mediterranean-style platters.

about the pub

The Grove
The Esplanade, Exmouth
Devon EX8 1BJ
Tel 01395 272101
www.youngs.co.uk

DIRECTIONS: from the car park follow signs through the town centre to the Esplanade
PARKING: none – on-street meter parking
OPEN: daily; all day
FOOD: daily; all day
BREWERY/COMPANY: Young's Brewery
REAL ALE: Young's Bitter, Special, seasonal beers

Family facilities

Children of all ages are welcome inside the pub and there's a family dining area and a children's menu as well as changing facilities for children.

Alternative refreshment stops

Exmouth has an extensive range of pubs and cafés to choose from. There's a café in Phear Park, the Dog and Donkey pub at the suggested turn-around point, or plenty of pubs and cafés in Budleigh Salterton if you choose to cycle on.

☛ Where to go from here

The World of Country Life at Sandy Bay is an all-weather family attraction where kids can meet friendly farm animals, view working models and exhibits from a bygone age, including steam and vintage vehicles, and enjoy a safari train ride through a 40-acre deer park (www.worldofcountrylife.co.uk). For exhilarating rides and huge indoor and outdoor play areas head for Crealy Adventure Park at Clyst St Mary (www.crealy.co.uk). See wholemeal flour being ground at an historic water-powered mill and various pottery, weaving and spinning studios at Otterton Mill (www.ottertonmill.com).

Bristol and Bath railway path

Park and ride with a difference, an easy ride to explore Bath's fine 18th-century architecture

Avon Valley Railway

The first section of the Avon Valley Railway opened in 1835, between Mangotsfield, just north of Warmley and Bristol. Originally a horse-drawn tramway, it transported local coal to Bristol. With growing industrialisation, the track was upgraded for steam and by 1869 had been extended all the way to Bath, following the course of the River Avon as it neared the city. After publication of the Beeching Report, passenger trains were withdrawn in March 1966, although goods traffic continued for a further five years, supplying coal to the gasworks in Bath. In 1972 the track was finally dismantled, but even as British Rail was removing the rails, the Bristol Suburban Railway Society was planning to reopen the line. A 2.5 mile (4km) section is now operational with extensions planned.

Known the world over for its Roman baths and elegant Cotswold-stone Georgian architecture, Bath simply demands exploration. Dedicated to the goddess Sulis, the baths were begun in the 1st century, the focus of a sophisticated city that thrived for nearly 400 years. After the Romans left, the baths were gradually forgotten and when Nash created his fashionable spa town, nobody even dreamed of their existence. The former complex was only rediscovered in 1880 when sewer works broke into the subterranean ruin, and subsequent excavation revealed the finest Roman remains in the country.

the ride

1 Leaving the car park adjacent to the former Warmley Station, go left to cross the main road at a traffic light controlled crossing and follow the path away beside the old signal box. Hidden behind the trees lining the path are small units, occupying the sites of the former industries that once supported the town. After passing beneath **St Ivel Way**, look for a sculpture that represents a Roman centurion quaffing wine from a flask: it recalls that a Roman road passed nearby. A little further along is a controlled crossing at **Victoria Road**.

2 Pedalling on brings you to **Oldland Common**, the northern terminus of the restored section of the Avon Valley Railway. The path continues beside the track, passing beneath North Street to enter a shallow cutting. The stone here, known as Pennant sandstone, is particularly hard and proved an excellent construction material. The excavated stone was used for several buildings in the vicinity. There are also coal deposits in the area, laid down during the same carboniferous period, and these

Left: The former Warmley Station

The elegant Pulteney Bridge over the River Avon in Bath

16

3h30 — 18.25 MILES — 29.4 KM — LEVEL 1 2 3

fuelled local brass foundries and other industries. Later on, at **Cherry Gardens**, the way enters a second cutting, exposing much younger rocks containing fossils of graptolites, belemnites and ammonites, creatures that lived in the Jurassic seas covering the region 200 million years ago. Before long, the **railway yard** at Bitton appears ahead, the cycle track swinging across the line through a gate (look out for passing trains) to reach the station.

3 Even if the trains are not running, there is always something of interest to see in the goods yard, with an assortment of engines and rolling stock either awaiting refurbishment or dismantling for spares. The buffet is generally open and for a small donation you are welcome to wander onto the platform. Go through the car park, over a small level crossing and continue beside the railway. Carry on along an embankment overlooking the Avon's flood meadows, crossing the river to reach **Avon Riverside Station**, where a path on the right drops to a picnic area by the water's edge.

4 At **Saltford**, the Bird in Hand below the embankment invites a break for refreshment. You can also wander into the village and have a look at the restored **Saltford Brass Mill**, which is open on some Saturdays during the summer months. Re-crossing the river the way continues towards Bath, the Avon winding below you twice more before you reach the outskirts of the city.

5 Eventually you emerge on **Brassmill Lane**. Follow the road to the right, keeping ahead on a short cycle lane further

MAP: OS Explorer 155 Bristol & Bath

START/FINISH: car park beside the A420 at Warmley, Kingswood; grid ref: ST670735

TRAILS/TRACKS: former railway line

LANDSCAPE: wooded cuttings and embankments with occasional views across riverside path into Bath

PUBLIC TOILETS: at car park at start

TOURIST INFORMATION: Bath, tel 01225 477101

CYCLE HIRE: Webbs of Warmley, High Street, Warmley, Bristol, tel 01179 673676

THE PUB: Bird in Hand, Saltford

! Traffic lights control major road crossings; dismount when crossing the restored railway line; take care when riding alongside the River Avon; route shared with pedestrians

Getting to the start

Warmley is on the A420 to the east of Bristol. The car park lies 0.25 mile (400m) east of the roundabout junction with the A4174.

Why do this cycle ride?

Bath is notorious for its traffic problems. For the cyclist, however, there is a splendid route along the track bed of the former Avon Valley Railway. It penetrates the heart of the city and has attractions of its own along the way: you can visit a brass mill, or ride along a section of the line, pulled by a vintage steam or diesel engine. The cycling is not strenuous, but for a shorter ride, turn around at Saltford.

Researched and written by: Dennis Kelsall

on past a 'no entry' sign for motorised traffic. Where the cycle lane ends, turn right (watch for oncoming traffic) to gain a riverside path behind a tool hire shop. Signed towards **Bath city centre**, keep going past the 19th-century industrial quarter of Bath, where more brass and other mills took advantage of the water for both power and transport. The factories have now gone, replaced by modern light industry, but some of the old riverside warehouses remain. The path finally ends near **Churchill Bridge** in the centre of Bath.

6 Although cyclists are common on Bath's streets, the traffic is busy and it is perhaps a good idea to find a convenient spot to secure your bikes whilst you explore on foot. When you are ready to head back, retrace your outward route to **Warmley** along the riverside path and cycleway.

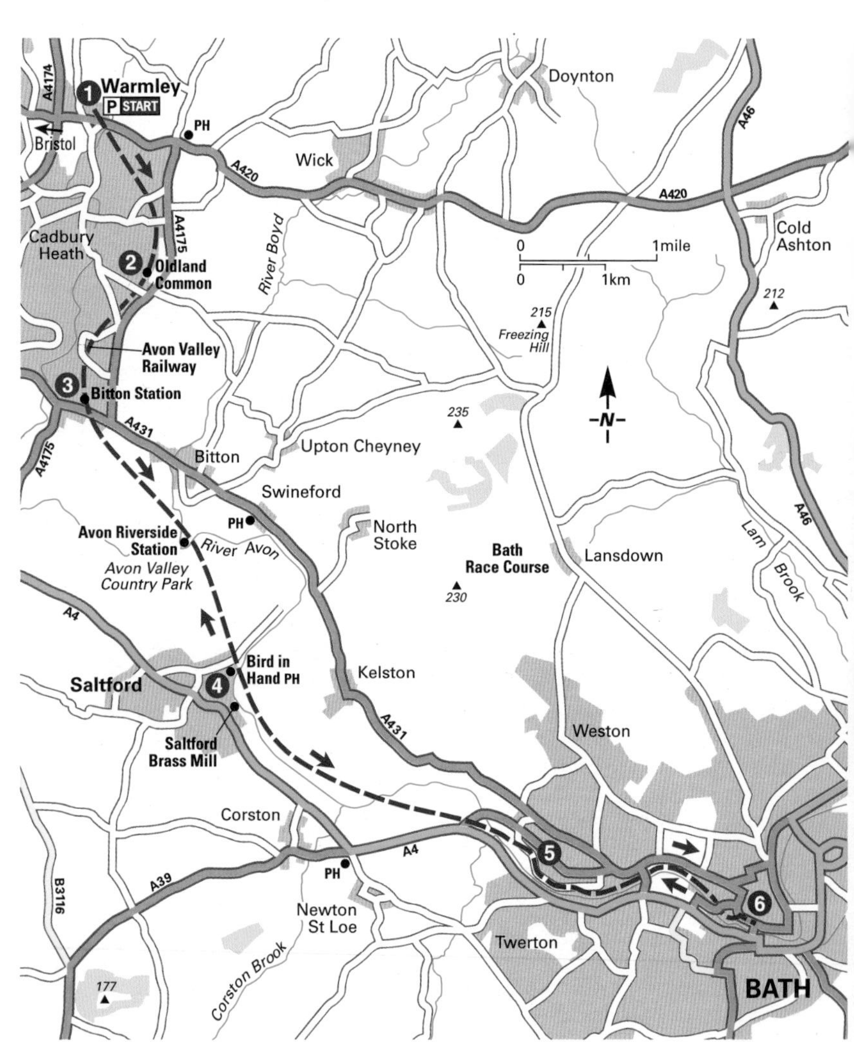

Bird in Hand

16

Converted in 1869 from two cottages in the original village close to the River Avon, the Bird in Hand first served the workers building the railway through the valley between Bath and Bristol. Now that the railway has gone, this homely village local, which is smack beside the old route, is a favoured resting and refuelling stop for cyclists pedalling the peaceful cycle path between the two cities. There's a comfortable bar area which is adorned with old pictures of the pub and village, a light and airy conservatory and plenty of outdoor seating for fine-weather eating and drinking.

Food

Lunchtime food ranges from Stilton ploughman's and salad platters to steak and ale pies, omelettes, and ham, egg and chips. Evening additions include a mixed grill and daily specials such as salmon fishcakes, sea bass with prawn and lemon butter sauce, dressed crab and rack of lamb with redcurrant and port sauce.

Family facilities

Children are very welcome in the family area, where a box of toys is provided to keep youngsters amused. There is a basic children's menu.

Alternative refreshment stops

There is an enormous range of pubs and cafés in Bath; café at Bitton Station.

☛ Where to go from here

Spend time in Bath visiting the Abbey, the Roman Baths and Pump Rooms (www.romanbaths.co.uk) or the excellent museums (www.bath-preservation-trust.org.uk). In Bristol head for the superb Zoo Gardens (www.bristolzoo.org.uk) or savour the unique sights, sounds and smells of steam trains along the Avon Valley Railway at Bitton (www.avonvalleyrailway.co.uk).

about the pub

Bird in Hand
58 High Street
Saltford, Bristol
BS31 3EN
Tel: 01225 873335

DIRECTIONS: 3 miles (4.8km) along the cycle track from Bitton railway station

PARKING: 36

OPEN: daily

FOOD: daily

BREWERY/COMPANY: free house

REAL ALE: Abbey Bellringer, Butcombe, Courage Best, guest beers

Stroud Valley cycle trail

Explore the Cotswolds' industrial heritage along a disused railway track.

Nailsworth valley

Throughout the medieval period, wool was an important product of the Cotswolds, much of it traded abroad as fleeces. However, it was only during the 17th century that workers around Stroud began to exploit the fast-flowing streams to power washing, dyeing and fulling mills. The valleys prospered as new inventions mechanised the spinning and weaving processes during the 18th century, and the canals, followed by the railways, provided a ready means of exporting the finished goods via the seaport of Bristol. At one time there were 15 mills spaced along the valley between Stonehouse and Nailsworth, but the age of steam, which initially contributed to their success, also heralded their gradual decline. The mills struggled to compete with the massive steam-driven factories on the coal fields of Lancashire and Yorkshire, and although some were modernised, the long-term cost of bringing in fuel proved uneconomic.

While operated as part of the Midland network, the Nailsworth Railway was completed in 1867 after 3 years' construction. It encouraged diversification of the mills into other products such as pin

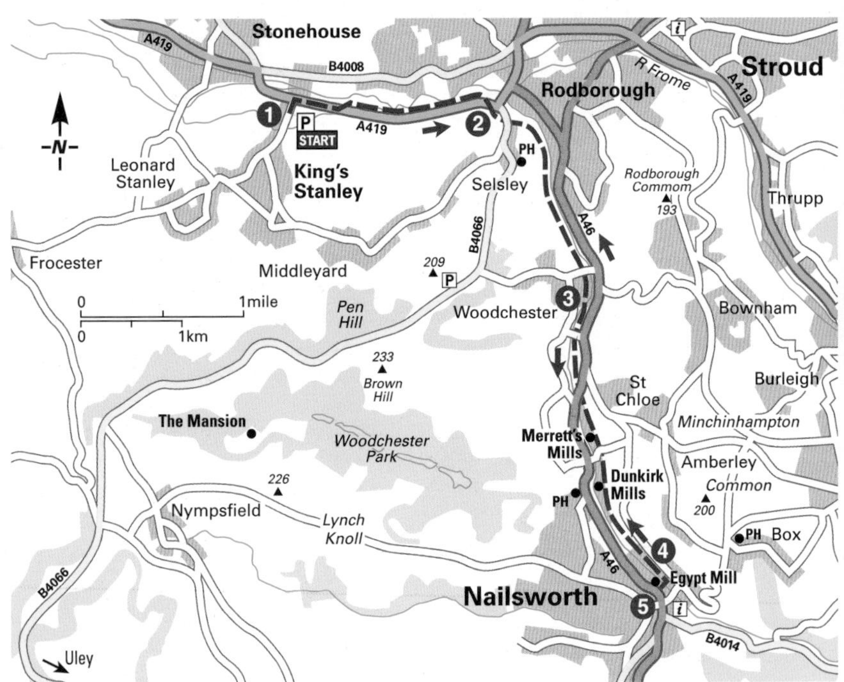

making, carpet manufacture, dye making and, of course, grain milling. One of the valley's more unusual products, walking sticks, are made from chestnut saplings, and the trade continues today, with Nailsworth claiming to be the largest producer in the world.

the ride

1 Leaving the car park, cross the King's Stanley road and then the A419 at the traffic lights. The **cycle way** runs briefly along the pavement in the direction of Dudbridge and Stroud, crossing another traffic light controlled junction at the entrance to a **small trading estate** – look both ways as you cross. Not far beyond, the track and road separate, the way continuing in pleasant seclusion between broad hedges. Breaks on the left allow occasional glimpses across the Frome valley, where meadows lie between the twisting river and the disused Stroudwater Canal. The route here is also a **miniature arboretum**, planted with intriguingly named varieties of apple and pear trees such as The Gillyflower of Gloucester, Chaxhill Red, Elison's Orange and Blakeney Red, developed during the 19th century for cider and perry manufacture as well as just for eating.

2 After a mile (1.6km), the track swings to cross the A419 next to the **Dudbridge roundabout** at pedestrian-controlled traffic lights. Go left on the far side, now following signs for Nailsworth, skirting the roundabout and entering a tunnel below the B4066. Keep ahead as you come out on the other side, the tree-lined track winding into the **Nailsworth Valley**. The stream that

2h00 · 9.5 MILES · 15.3 KM · LEVEL 123

MAP: OS Explorer 168 Stroud, Tetbury & Malmesbury

START/FINISH: car park beside A419 at King's Stanley; grid ref: SO814044

TRAILS/TRACKS: firm track

LANDSCAPE: disused railway track following the course of the River Frome and the Nailsworth Valley

PUBLIC TOILETS: none on route

TOURIST INFORMATION: Nailsworth, tel 01453 839222

CYCLE HIRE: None locally

THE PUB: Egypt Mill, Nailsworth

! Major road crossings controlled by traffic lights, shared with pedestrians

Getting to the start

Stroud is 8 miles (12.9km) south of Gloucester. The ride begins from a car park at the edge of Stonehouse beside a junction on the A419, where an unclassified road leaves south to King's Stanley.

Why do this cycle ride?

The deep, steep-sided valleys converging on Stroud have a very different character to the rolling wolds further north. Canals and railways guaranteed prosperity into the 19th century, providing ready access to formerly remote areas. This easy ride follows the course of the former Nailsworth Railway from Stonehouse, at one time lined with a succession of busy mills.

Researched and written by:
Dennis Kelsall, Christopher Knowles

powered the many mills along its course runs beside you, seemingly altogether too insignificant for the work demanded from it. Its force was concentrated by damming small ponds or lodges at intervals. Look out for a sudden dip where a bridge over a crossing track has been removed, then after passing beneath a bridge, go over a residential street.

3 The track shortly crosses **Nailsworth Stream**, then briefly runs beside the main road before reaching Station Road. There is little to mark the former station as the trail continues, in a little distance passing beneath the main road and then beside **Merrett's Mills**, now occupied by industrial units. As the railings finish beyond it, keep an eye open for a small bridge taking the track over a narrow path. The path, reached on the left just after crossing, provides pedestrian access to **Dunkirk Mills**. Although now largely converted to residential accommodation, it houses a small museum, which is occasionally open in summer and contains working machinery from the former textile mill. The track continues through trees along the valley, past the lodges that created a head of water for driving the mill wheels, and eventually reaches a residential development and car park at **Goldwater Springs**.

4 Follow the access drive out to the left, swinging right to follow a lane past a fire station. Just before crossing a bridge to meet the main road into Nailsworth, go right again into **Egypt Mill**. Another of the valley's former industrial mills, it is enjoying a new career as a hotel. Inside, it retains two original mill wheels and their gearing in working order, and they can be seen from the basement bars, turning in the flow.

5 In the past, the abrupt sides of the valley kept Nailsworth relatively isolated from the outside world. This means that, without tackling the steep hills onto Minchinhampton Common, the only return route is back the way you came.

The river near Egypt Mill, prettily surrounded by bushes, plants and trees

Egypt Mill

17

Stroud Valley GLOUCESTERSHIRE

about the pub

Egypt Mill
Nailsworth, Stroud
Gloucestershire GL6 0AE
Tel: 01453 833449

DIRECTIONS: first right at roundabout, then left on leaving the A46 heading north out of Nailsworth towards Stroud

PARKING: 60

OPEN: daily; all day

FOOD: daily

BREWERY/COMPANY: free house

REAL ALE: Archer's Best; guest beer in summer

ROOMS: 28 en suite

Situated in the charming Cotswold town of Nailsworth, this smartly converted 16th-century corn mill contains many features of great character, including two working water wheels, the original millstones and lifting equipment. The refurbished, split-level ground floor bar and bistro are informal, offering a relaxing atmosphere and super views of the water wheels and over the pretty millstream to the peaceful water gardens. The large and very comfortable Egypt Mill Lounge sports stripped beams and old mill machinery ironwork. There's a choice of eating in the bistro or restaurant, and in both there is a good selection of wines by the glass. Bedrooms are well equipped and tastefully furnished.

Food

Light lunches range from sandwiches and ciabatta rolls (bacon and Brie) served with salad and crisps, risottos and salads, cheeses and cold meats, pasta dishes and local sausages and mash. The main menu may take in starters such as deep-fried spicy crab cakes, smoked salmon, or portobello mushrooms, followed by confit of duck leg, deep-fried haddock or steak and kidney suet pudding. Round off with toffee and pecan nut tart or lemon and vanilla New York baked cheesecake.

Family facilities

Children are very welcome in the bars and overnight (family room with cots). There's a children's menu and plenty of summer seating in the riverside gardens, where young children must be supervised.

Alternative refreshment stops

Choice of pubs in Nailsworth.

☛ Where to go from here

See working machinery and historical displays at the Dunkirk Mill Centre, a fulling mill demonstrating the finishing of fine woollen cloth (www.stroud-textile.org.uk). View dinosaur remains and a Roman temple at the Museum in the Park in Stroud (www.stroud.gov.uk). Explore Owlpen Manor, a romantic Tudor manor with formal yew gardens (www.owlpen.com) or the unfinished Woodchester Mansion (www.woodchestermansion.org.uk).

From Bradford-on-Avon along the Kennet & Avon Canal

Discover one of Brindley's great canal masterpieces.

Kennet & Avon Canal

John Rennie began the construction of the Kennet and Avon Canal in 1794 to link the Avon and Kennet Navigations between Bath and Bristol and thus create a continuous waterway between Bristol and London. The 57 mile (92km) canal took 16 years to complete and was quite an achievement, requiring two great aqueducts and a spectacular flight of 29 locks at Caen Hill outside Devizes to lift the waterway over 240ft (73m) onto the summit level. It proved a highly profitable venture and was soon carrying over 350,000 tons a year between the two great cities. By the middle of the 19th century, competition from railways foreshadowed its decline, and in 1846 it was taken over by the Great Western Railway Company. GWR signs remain on some of its bridges, ominously mounted on the instrument of its ruin, an upended length of railway track. Re-opened in 1990, many of the canal's original features still excite the imagination, none more so than the two splendid stone aqueducts carrying the canal across the Avon Valley, one of them named after the canal company's founding chairman, Charles Dundas. They presented major technical difficulties for Rennie as they had not only to carry a great weight but remain watertight, yet in the

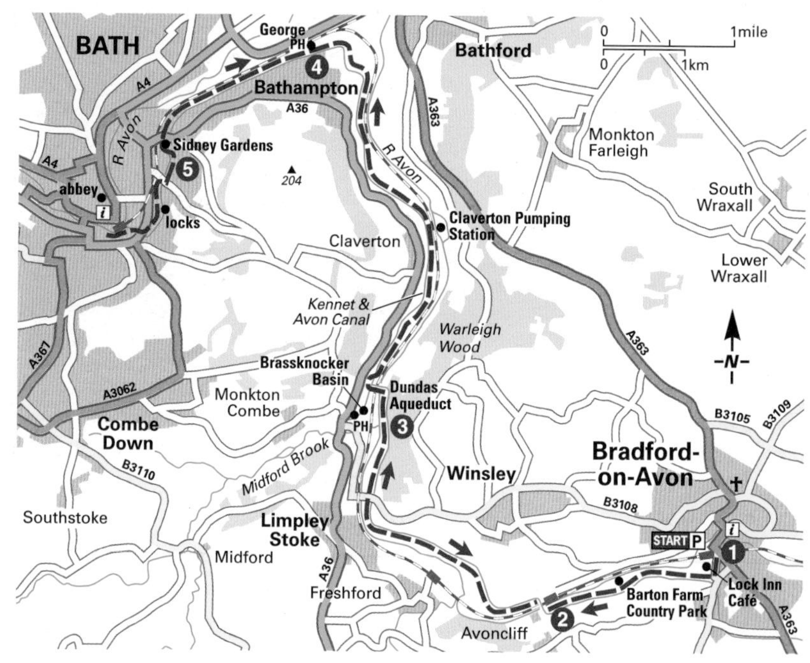

Dundas Aqueduct, where the Kennet and Avon Canal turns sharply

18

4h00 — 20 MILES — 32.2 KM — LEVEL 1 2 3

SHORTER ALTERNATIVE ROUTE

3h00 — 15 MILES — 24.1 KM — LEVEL 1 2 3

MAP: OS Explorer 155 Bristol & Bath & 156 Chippenham & Bradford-on-Avon

START/FINISH: Bradford-on-Avon railway station (pay car park); grid ref: ST825606

TRAILS/TRACKS: gravel towpath, short section on road

LANDSCAPE: canal towpath through the wooded and pastoral Avon Valley

PUBLIC TOILETS: at start

TOURIST INFORMATION: Bradford-on-Avon, tel 01225 865797

CYCLE HIRE: The Lock Inn Café, 48 Frome Road, Bradford-on-Avon tel: 01225 868068

THE PUB: The George, Bathampton

! Care through town; unguarded canal towpaths shared with pedestrians; blind approaches to bridges; dismount in tunnels; flight of steps on approaching Bath

Getting to the start

Bradford-on-Avon is only 5 miles (8km) south east of Bath and lies on the A363 to Trowbridge. Park at the railway station, from where the ride begins.

Why do this cycle ride?

The Kennet and Avon Canal passes through picturesque countryside. The attractive riverside pub at Bathampton offers a turning point although the locks passed into Bath on the longer ride are worth seeing.

Researched and written by: Dennis Kelsall

best tradition of the great architects, his creations managed to combine both aesthetic quality and practicality.

the ride

1 Leaving the station car park, turn right along the main road in the direction of Frome. Continue past a mini-roundabout to the Canal Tavern and Lock Inn Café. Go between them to join the towpath and follow it past **Grange Farm** with its massive 600-year-old tithe barn. The River Avon runs below to the right, containing Barton Farm Country Park's picnic and wildlife areas within the intervening spit of land. Beyond a gate, continue beside the canal to **Avoncliff**.

2 The canal now makes an abrupt turn across the Avon Valley, carried above both the river and railway on an imposing aqueduct. Do not cross, but at a sign to Dundas just before, drop steeply right towards the **Cross Guns** pub, then double back left underneath the bridge, climbing left to gain the opposite towpath. Tacked along the wooded valley, the waterway runs pleasantly on, harbouring an assortment of ducks, coots and moorhens. Turning a corner opposite **Limpley Stoke**, pass beneath a road bridge, then look out on the left for a glimpse of a viaduct taking the A36 across the Midford Brook valley.

Taking life at a leisurely pace along the canal

3 Another sharp turn heralds the **Dundas Aqueduct**, immediately beyond which is the last remnant of the Somerset Coal Canal, completed in 1805 to transport coal from Radstock and Paulton to Bristol. The track just before it leads to **Brassknocker Basin**, where a small exhibition (open daily in summer) describes its history. The route, however, continues ahead, signed 'Bath and Claverton', winding behind a **derrick** and maintenance building and on to the opposite bank. A mile (1.2km) further on, immediately beyond a bridge, a track drops across the railway to the river where there is a restored pump house (**Claverton Pumping Station**), built in 1813 to replenish the water drained by the locks descending to Bath. There are views to Bathford and Batheaston as you pedal the last 1.75 miles (2.8km) to **Bathampton** and The George.

4 To extend the ride, continue beside the canal, the eastern suburbs of Bath rising on the opposite side of the valley. Eventually the city itself comes into view with a glimpse of the abbey at its heart. There are a couple of short tunnels to pass through at **Sidney Gardens**, where you should dismount. Between them, two **ornate cast-iron bridges** span the canal, which, together with the elaborate façade of the second tunnel beneath Cleveland House, were added to placate the owners of Sidney Park, who rather disapproved of common cargo barges passing through their land.

5 Emerging below **Cleveland House**, the towpath doubles back onto the opposite bank, passes former warehouses, now a **marina**, and rises to a road. Taking care, diagonally cross and drop back to the towpath, here having to negotiate a flight of steps. Beyond, the canal falls impressively through a succession of locks, the path periodically rising to cross a couple of roads and a track before meeting the River Avon. To explore Bath, carry on a little further by the river to emerge on the road beside **Churchill Bridge** in the city centre. As the city is busy, it is perhaps preferable to secure your bikes whilst you wander around. The return is back the way you came, but remember you have to climb steps to the road at Bathwick Hill and dismount through the tunnels at Sidney Gardens, or you could return by train.

The George

The pub's enviable position by the parish church and a bridge over the Kennet and Avon Canal is one of its attractions. The creeper-clad building is so close to the water that the entrance to the upper dining room is from the towpath. When the weather is fine, the tables on the canalside terrace fill quickly with walkers, cyclists and barge visitors, and you can watch the many activities on the canal. Inside, there's a warren of wood-beamed rooms radiating out from the flagstoned central bar, with plenty of space away from the bar for families. The George oozes history, dating back to the 13th century when it was originally a monastery. The last official duel in England was fought on nearby Claverton Down in 1778 following a quarrel over a game of cards at The George. The fatally wounded Viscount du Barré was buried in the churchyard opposite.

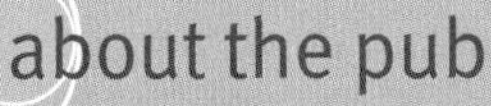

about the pub

The George
Mill Lane
Bathampton, Bath
Bath & NE Somerset BA2 6TR
Tel: 01225 425079

DIRECTIONS: at Bathampton on the A36 east of Bath, take minor road left downhill to village centre, crossing the canal to the church. The George is beside the canal near the church

PARKING: 50

OPEN: daily; all day

FOOD: daily; all day

BREWERY/COMPANY: Chef & Brewer

REAL ALE: Courage Best, Directors and a changing guest ale

Food

Expect traditional pub food – sandwiches, baguettes and filled rolls, salads, ploughman's lunches, and changing blackboard specials, perhaps roast monkfish, steak and kidney pudding or Tuscan-style swordfish.

Family facilities

Children are welcome away from the bar and a children's menu is available. Keep an eye on children on the canalside terrace.

Alternative refreshment stops

Plenty of eating places in Bradford-on-Avon and Bath. The Lock Inn Café near the start, the Cross Guns at Avoncliff, the Hop Pole and a canalside tea room at Limpley Stoke.

☛ Where to go from here

Take a closer look at the tithe barn and seek out the unspoiled Saxon church in Bradford-on-Avon. Visit the Claverton Pumping Station (www.claverton.org) or explore Bath's famous buildings and museums (www.bath-preservation-trust.org.uk). Peto Gardens at Iford Manor (www.ifordarts.co.uk) are worth seeing.

19

Malmesbury and the Fosse Way

Visit the splendid remnants of an ancient abbey church and follow in the footsteps of Roman soldiers.

Malmesbury Abbey

All that is left of Malmesbury's great monastery, founded in 676 by St Aldhelm, is part of the abbey church, which survived Henry VIII's Dissolution only because it was granted to the town for use as its parish church. The building dates from the 12th century and was constructed on a vast cruciform plan. Beside it stood a secluded cloister surrounded by the domestic buildings in which the monks lived.

If what remains is anything to go by, then the medieval building must have been a truly magnificent sight, a long avenue of soaring columns lifting the roof high above the church. Exquisite stonework is revealed in fine arches, vaulting and tracery, while the early Norman carving in the porch is particularly striking.

An unusual and rare feature is the curious watching loft that projects from the upper wall, high above the southern side of the nave; nobody is really sure what purpose it served. Also of interest is the tomb of Alfred the Great's grandson, King Athelstan. He commissioned the first translation of the Bible into English, and his tomb stands near the north west corner of the church, while outside is the grave of Hannah Twynnoy, a servant at the town's White Lion Inn, who died after being mauled by a tiger in 1703.

the ride

1 Out of The Vine Tree car park, pedal easily away along the lane to the left, reaching a junction after 0.75 mile (1.2km). Keep left with the main lane, before long

arriving at **Foxley**. Go right, passing the community's tiny church.

2 Continue along the lane for 2 miles (3.2km) to the outskirts of Malmesbury, where **Common Road** joins from the right. Keep going as the road shortly winds down to cross the Sherston branch of the River Avon, where there is a view right to the **abbey church**. Climb away, remaining with the main road as it bends right to a T-junction. Go right, and then at the next junction, in front of The Triangle and **war memorial,** go right again to the abbey. It is perhaps a good idea to park your bike there while you explore the town centre, just a short walk away.

3 Ride back to the junction by the war memorial and now turn right along Gloucester Road, passing through the town to a mini-roundabout. There, bear left into Park Road, signed to **Park Road Industrial Estate**. Fork off right after 300yds (274m) to remain with Park Road. After passing a few more houses, the route abruptly leaves the town, and continues beside the Avon's **Tetbury Branch** along a narrow hedged lane.

4 Reaching a T-junction, go right, crossing the river towards **Brokenborough**. The lane climbs easily to the village, passing the **Rose and Crown** and then falling to the church and Church Lane. After 100yds (91m), turn off left into a lane marked as a cul-de-sac. After dropping to re-cross the river, the narrow lane climbs past **Brook Farm**, initially steeply, but soon levelling to continue between the fields.

19

2h00 · 9.75 MILES · 15.7 KM · LEVEL 123

MAP: OS Explorer 168 Stroud, Tetbury & Malmesbury

START/FINISH: The Vine Tree, Norton (ask permission first); grid ref: ST887846

TRAILS/TRACKS: country lanes and gravel tracks, a short town section at Malmesbury

LANDSCAPE: undulating hill farmland

PUBLIC TOILETS: in Malmesbury behind the town square

TOURIST INFORMATION: Malmesbury; tel: 01666 823748

CYCLE HIRE: C H White & Son, 51 High Street, Malmesbury, tel 01666 822330 (prior bookings only) – alternative start

THE PUB: The Vine Tree, Norton

! Great care to be taken through Malmesbury; steep descent and climb at Roman Bridge on the Fosse Way

Getting to the start

Malmesbury stands midway between Chippenham and Cirencester just off the A429 on the B4040. Norton is 3 miles (4.8km) to the south west . On entering the village, turn right, signposted Foxley, follow the road round to the right for the pub.

Why do this cycle ride?

This undemanding ride combines historic Malmesbury with quiet lanes and good off-road cycling. The route roughly follows part of two shallow valleys which converge on Malmesbury. The 'circle' is completed along a straight stretch of the Fosse Way.

Researched and written by: Dennis Kelsall

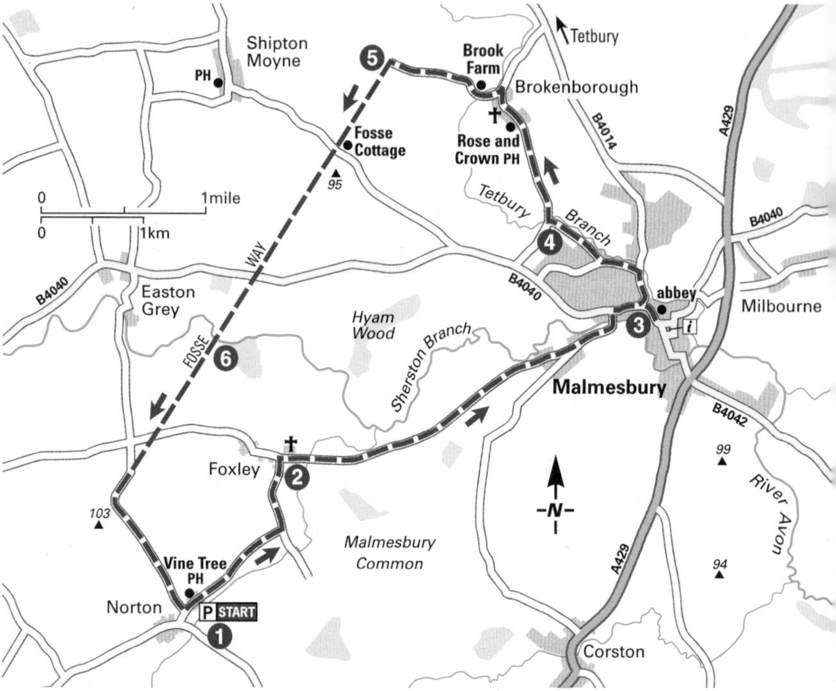

5 The track ends at a T-junction with a broad, straight track, the **Fosse Way**. Go left. Very soon, the tarmac gives way to coarse gravel and stone, and although the way is firm, the surface is loose in places and there is a risk of skidding if you travel at speed. After 0.5 mile (800m), cross a lane by **Fosse Cottage** and carry on past a water-pumping station for another mile (1.6km) to the B4040. Keep an eye open for fast-moving traffic as you cross and continue, the track, before long, starting a steepening descent. It bends at the bottom to a bridge over the **Sherston Branch**.

6 Although widened in modern times the upstream portion of the bridge is original and dates back to a Roman settlement beside the river. The climb away on the far bank is very steep, and you may have to get off and push. Beyond, the way runs easily again for 0.5 mile (800m) to another road crossing. Keep ahead with the byway, the surface now of earth and a little rutted, shortly emerging onto another lane. Go ahead, staying with it as it soon bends left away from the line of the Roman road. Eventually dropping to a T-junction at the edge of **Norton**, go left to The Vine Tree.

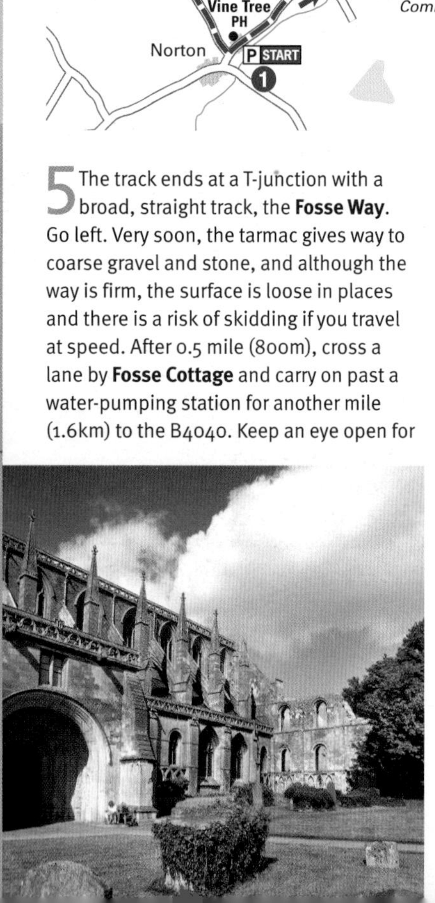

The south view of the remnants of Malmesbury Abbey

The Vine Tree

The Vine Tree is a converted 16th-century mill house close to Westonbirt Arboretum, and is well worth seeking out for its interesting modern pub food and memorable outdoor summer dining. The tranquil sun-trap terrace includes a fountain, lavender hedge, pagodas, trailing vines and a barbecue. There's also a 2 acre (0.8ha) garden with a play area, and two boules pitches. If the weather is wet, be consoled with a pint of Fiddlers Elbow by the log fire in the main bar, with its old oak beams and flagstone floors. As well as a changing selection of real ales, there's a carefully selected list of wines (up to 30 by the glass), and decent coffee. Cooking is modern British, everything is made on the premises, and meals are served in the pine-furnished dining areas.

Food

The menu changes daily and closely follows the seasons, using local produce wherever possible. Choose from light bites (smoked haddock kedgeree, roast Cotswold pork baguette) and vegetarian options (wild mushroom and feta risotto) or trio of local award-winning sausages with bubble and squeak and a grain mustard sauce, or gilt-head bream with lemongrass and sweet basil broth. Imaginative puddings.

Family facilities

Well-behaved children are welcome in the pub. High chairs are at hand, a children's menu, including home-made chicken nuggets, is available as are smaller portions, plus colouring equipment to keep youngsters amused. Sun-trap terrace and a huge garden/field with play area and space for impromptu football and cricket.

about the pub

The Vine Tree
Foxley Road, Norton
Malmesbury, Wiltshire SN16 0JP
Tel: 01666 837654
www.thevinetree.co.uk

DIRECTIONS: see Getting to the Start

PARKING: 100

OPEN: daily; all day Sunday

FOOD: daily; all day Sunday (& Saturday if fine) in summer

BREWERY/COMPANY: free house

REAL ALE: Butcombe Bitter, Tinners and guest beers

Alternative refreshment stops

Various pubs and cafés in Malmesbury; the Rose & Crown at Brokenborough

☛ Where to go from here

Visit the impressive remains of Malmesbury's Benedictine abbey, and in the spring and summer visit the Abbey House Gardens (www.abbeyhousegardens.co.uk). In nearby Tetbury the Police Museum (www.tetbury.org) explains how policing was carried out in the early 1900s.

20

Holt WILTSHIRE

Between Holt and Lacock

Gardens, a 15th-century house and a former abbey are highlights that await discovery on this ride.

Two great manors

Holt's lovely gardens, surrounding an 18th-century house, were laid out in the early 1900s by Sir George Hastings, who set out to combine formal composition with corners of natural beauty. The house, which is not open to the public, is built upon a former textile mill, and is known as 'The Courts', for it was here that disputes were once brought for settlement.

Constructed in 1480 by Thomas Tropnell on the site of an earlier fortified manor, from which the moat and defensive foundations survive, Great Chalfield is a wonderful example of the architecture of its period, when comfort and decoration were assuming precedence over the Spartan necessities of protection. In creating his manor house, Tropnell also made alterations to the adjacent church, adding a chapel on its south side. It is entered through a finely carved stone screen portraying the heraldry of the Tropnell family. Another interesting feature is a three-decker pulpit, above which is a wooden canopy, a sounding board to project the speaker's voice.

Both properties belong to the National Trust, as does Lacock Abbey.

the ride

1 From the car park, cycle onto the main street and follow it right, shortly turning right again into **Leigh Road** opposite The Tollgate Inn. The way is signed to Great Chalfield. After less than 0.5 mile (800m), fork off right onto a lesser lane, passing through the parkland surrounding **Holt Manor**. At the end turn right yet again, the lane eventually winding around to **Great Chalfield Manor**.

2 Swing right opposite the entrance, joining a gently rising avenue that before long leads to a T-junction. At this point, if you wish to do the shorter ride, go left and at the crossroads, go left again to pick up the return instructions at Point 7. Otherwise, turn right to reach **Broughton Gifford**. Carry on, passing **The Bell** at the far side of the village to then fork left towards Melksham. After 0.33 mile (500m), go left beside a cottage into **Norrington Lane**. At its eventual end go right along the A365, dropping to traffic lights by **Shaw church**. Turn left along the B3353 towards Corsham and keep going to leave Whitley behind,

Left: Great Chalfield church beyond a pond

until you arrive at a turning off on the right, where the road bends to the left.

3 At this point you have a choice, and can cut off a corner by following a bridlepath. However, after rain the way can be muddy, and its uneven nature may render it unsuitable for very young or inexperienced riders. The alternative is to carry on along the road to **Gastard** and turn right into Lanes End opposite the **Harp and Crown**. Follow it out of the village, continuing past lesser lanes on the left, eventually arriving at the point at which the short cut joins from the right.

For the short cut, turn right along Westlands Lane, and after the houses finish, look for adjacent gates on the left, almost opposite **farm buildings**. Pass through the rightmost one of the two and follow the left-hand field-edge to the corner. Through another gate a grassy path drops into trees, continuing as a narrow hedged way. It soon widens and later, by **Catridge Farm**, joins a tarmac drive, which at its far end meets a lane. Go right.

4 Follow the lane to the A350. Dismount and cross with care to a gap in the opposite hedge. Continue along a short street to a mini-roundabout at the edge of Lacock. Bear left into the village, then turn right to **Lacock Abbey** and **The Red Lion**.

5 Return to the main street and turn right, passing **The George Inn** to leave the village and meet the A350 once more at traffic lights, which enable you to cross. Go right and then immediately left towards **Notton**. Stay with the main lane for 2 miles (3.2km), crossing a couple of railway

3h30 | 10 MILES | 28.1 KM | LEVEL 2

SHORTER ALTERNATIVE ROUTE

1h30 | 6.25 MILES | 17.5 KM | LEVEL 2

MAP: OS Explorer 156 Chippenham & Bradford-on-Avon

START/FINISH: Car park in Holt; grid ref: ST861619

TRAILS/TRACKS: lanes and quiet roads, short section on a main road, one off-road section that can be avoided

LANDSCAPE: low-lying hills bordering the Avon valley

PUBLIC TOILETS: at car park opposite the entrance to The Courts Garden

TOURIST INFORMATION: Melksham, tel 01225 707424

CYCLE HIRE: none locally

THE PUB: The Red Lion, Lacock

! Care crossing main road at Lacock; initial section of bridleway cut-through may be difficult after wet weather, or for inexperienced riders

Getting to the start

Holt lies between Melksham and Bradford-on-Avon on the B3107.

Why do this cycle ride?

Although a long ride, the hills are gentle and there is easy cycling and much to see. The circuit begins at Holt, whilst only a couple of miles (3.2km) away is a charming 15th-century house. As you return the route passes through Lacock. A much shorter ride is possible, linking Holt and Great Chalfield.

Researched and written by: Dennis Kelsall

bridges. Shortly after the second bridge, take the first turning off left, **Ladbrook Lane**, signed to Neston. It drops past the cemetery then re-crosses the railway, rising beyond and eventually reaching a crossroads.

6 Straight over, continue climbing past **Monk's Park**, at the top, turning sharp right to **Neston**. Keep ahead until you reach a fork and there bear left. Steadily losing height, carry on towards **Atworth**. Where the lane ends at the A365, go left and then almost immediately right, bearing left with the main lane as you leave the village towards **Stonar.** The shorter route rejoins from the left at a minor crossroads after 0.75 mile (1.2km).

7 Keep ahead to a fork and bear left, following the lane all the way back to Holt. Turn left in front of **The Tollgate Inn** to return through the village to the car park.

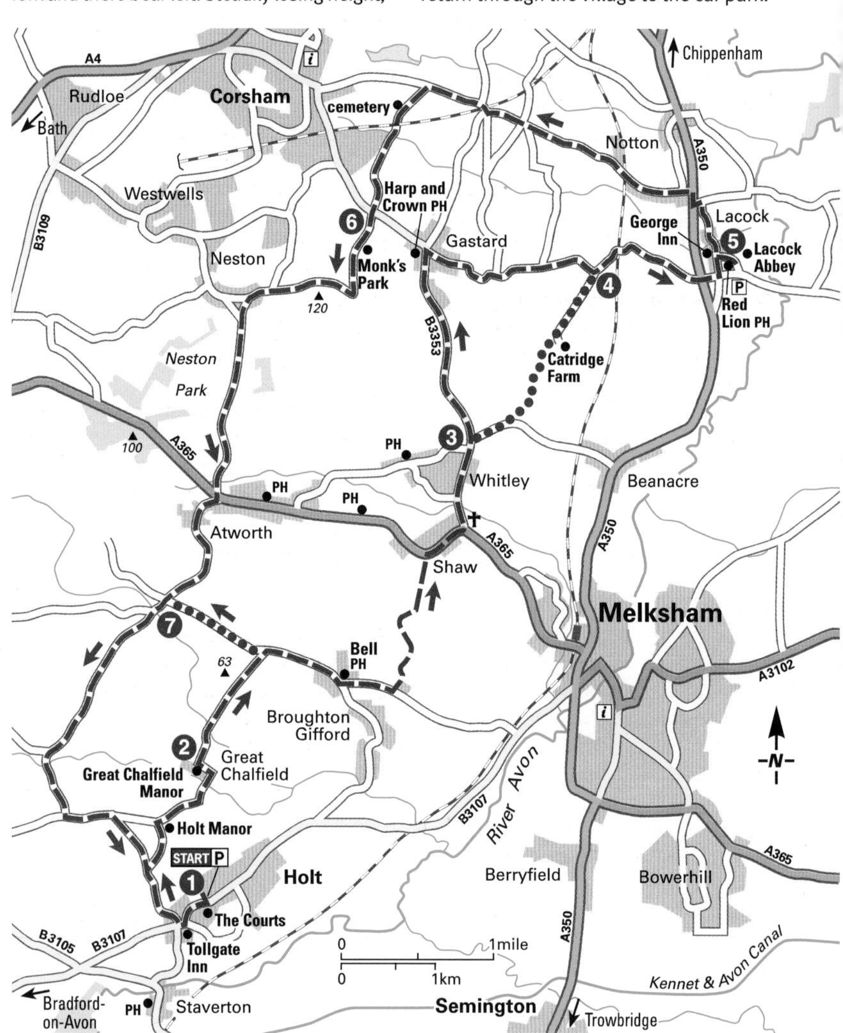

The Red Lion

20

Set in the centre of this famous National Trust village, immortalised in many a TV and film recording, the Red Lion is a tall, imposing red-brick Georgian coaching inn that has managed to retain its traditional character despite the crowds of tourists. Inside the three rambling, interconnecting bars there is plenty to catch the eye, from the old beams and the crackling log fires to the collections of farming implements, old oil paintings and the sturdy old furnishings on rug-strewn flagstone and bare board floors. A great place to relax after exploring the village, with excellent Wadworth ales on tap, and a sheltered, gravelled rear courtyard garden with abundant shrubs, flowers and picnic benches. Comfortable accommodation in period furnished bedrooms.

about the pub

The Red Lion
High Street, Lacock
Chippenham, Wiltshire SN15 2LQ
Tel: 01249 730456

DIRECTIONS: situated opposite the entrance to Lacock Abbey in the village centre

PARKING: 70

OPEN: daily

FOOD: daily

BREWERY/COMPANY: Wadworth Brewery

REAL ALE: Wadworth 6X, Henry's IPA, JCB and seasonal beers

ROOMS: 5 en suite

Food

Good bar food ranges from traditional snacks such as home-made soup and bread, decent ploughman's lunches and sandwiches on a printed menu to daily blackboard specials, perhaps steak and kidney pie, venison steak with red wine sauce, and lamb and apricot casserole.

Family facilities

Families are made very welcome, the rambling interior having plenty of secluded areas for children. There's a separate menu for younger children to choose from.

Alternative refreshment stops

In Holt you have the choice of the Old Ham Tree or the Tollgate Inn (children over 10 only). There are tea rooms and The George Inn in Lacock. Along the way are the Bell at Broughton Gifford and the Harp and Crown in Gastard.

☛ Where to go from here

Explore the attractive gardens at The Courts in Holt and make time to visit the enchanting Great Chalfield Manor, one of the most perfect examples of the late medieval English manor house. Lacock Abbey and the Fox Talbot Museum (photography) are also worth visiting. The National Trust's website (www.nationaltrust.org.uk) has information about all these attractions.

21

Around Sapperton

Above the valley of the River Frome and through the Earl of Bathurst's estate.

Sapperton church

There are few churches dedicated to St Kenelm, an historical figure and mentioned in *The Canterbury Tales*, but Sapperton's is one. Heir to the throne of Mercia, Kenelm's kingdom was thrust upon him by the untimely death of his father in 819 when he was only eight years old. However, his elder sister wanted the crown for herself and persuaded the lad's guardian to murder him. The treachery was exposed in a parchment miraculously conveyed to the pope in Rome by a dove, and Kenelm's body was recovered and taken to Winchcombe Abbey for burial. At the spot where his body was rested each night on its journey, a healing spring is said to have sprouted from the ground.

Go inside Sapperton's church and you might find it something of a surprise, for although of ancient foundation it was substantially rebuilt in the airy style of the 18th century by the Atkyns family of Sapperton Manor. Inside are several splendid features, including a funerary tableau depicting Sir Henry Pool with his wife Anne and their children. So fine is the work that even the half-turned pages of their missals appear real. The tiny St Michael's Church at Duntisbourne Rouse is also not to be missed, for it has a beautiful Saxon doorway and striking herringbone work in its walls. Within are wall paintings from the 13th century and misericords that are believed to have been brought from the abbey at Cirencester.

the ride

1 Emerging from the cul-de-sac lane by **St Kenelm's Church**, turn left up the hill, passing The Bell. The gradient soon eases as the way approaches a junction, at which go left again. There follows a pleasant 3 miles (4.8km) along the high ground above the Frome valley, passing **Parkcorner Farm**, **Gloucester Lodge**, one of the gates into the Cirencester Park estate, and, later, **Jackbarrow Farm**.

2 There is an opportunity to shorten the ride at this point, by cutting right to **Duntisbourne Abbots** and turning right in the village at a sign to the church.

A steeply curving road through the Cotswold-stone Duntisbourne Abbots

2h45 | 14 MILES | 22.5 KM | LEVEL 123

Otherwise, carry on ahead for a further 1.5 miles (2.4km), the road narrower and signed 'Winstone and Cheltenham'. Approaching **Winstone**, the lane bends sharply right into the village. After passing roadside farmhouses, bend left towards **Elkstone** and **Birdslip**, very soon reaching a crossroads beyond the village hall.

3 Now following a sign to Cirencester, keep ahead out of Winstone, where a fold in the open vista on the right conceals the head of the Duntisbourne valley. Before long, the lane turns abruptly right beside the **A417** trunk road, which follows the line of the Roman Ermine Way that once ran along between Corinium (Cirencester) and Calleva Atrebatum (Silchester). Cycle down to a junction by a bridge.

4 The onward route lies ahead, but to reach **The Five Mile House**, turn left through the underpass and then go right. Come back to this point to continue the ride, climbing in the direction of **Duntisbourne Abbots**. At the end go right, beyond a rise, the lane dropping into the village. However, control the speed of your descent, for there is a tight bend at the bottom of the hill. Climb to a junction and there go left to the church.

5 Follow the lane around **the church**, then turn sharp left to a second junction by a telephone box. The narrow lane to the right leads to a ford that follows the streambed a short distance, a causeway beside it offering a dry-shod crossing. Remounting beyond, carry on to a junction, go right and then left, leaving towards **Middle Duntisbourne** and **Daglingworth**. The way

MAP: OS Explorer 168 Stroud, Tetbury & Malmesbury & 179 Gloucester, Cheltenham & Stroud

START/FINISH: Sapperton: roadside parking beside the church; grid ref SO947033

TRAILS/TRACKS: country lanes

LANDSCAPE: patterned fields and woodland

PUBLIC TOILETS: none on route

TOURIST INFORMATION: Cirencester, tel 01285 654180

CYCLE HIRE: none locally

THE PUB: The Five Mile House, Duntisbourne Abbots

! Care on narrow lanes; dismount to cross ford

Getting to the start

Perched on the brim of the River Frome's narrow valley, Sapperton lies some 7 miles (11.3km) east of Stroud. The A419 to Cirencester passes just south of the village, and entering via minor lanes you will find roadside parking at the start of the ride in a cul-de-sac beside the church.

Why do this cycle ride?

It is difficult to go far in the Cotswolds without encountering steep hills, but at Sapperton, the rise and fall of the terrain is relatively gentle, offering mostly easy cycling along quiet lanes. The route describes a loop through several attractive villages, returning across part of Cirencester Park.

Researched and written by: Dennis Kelsall

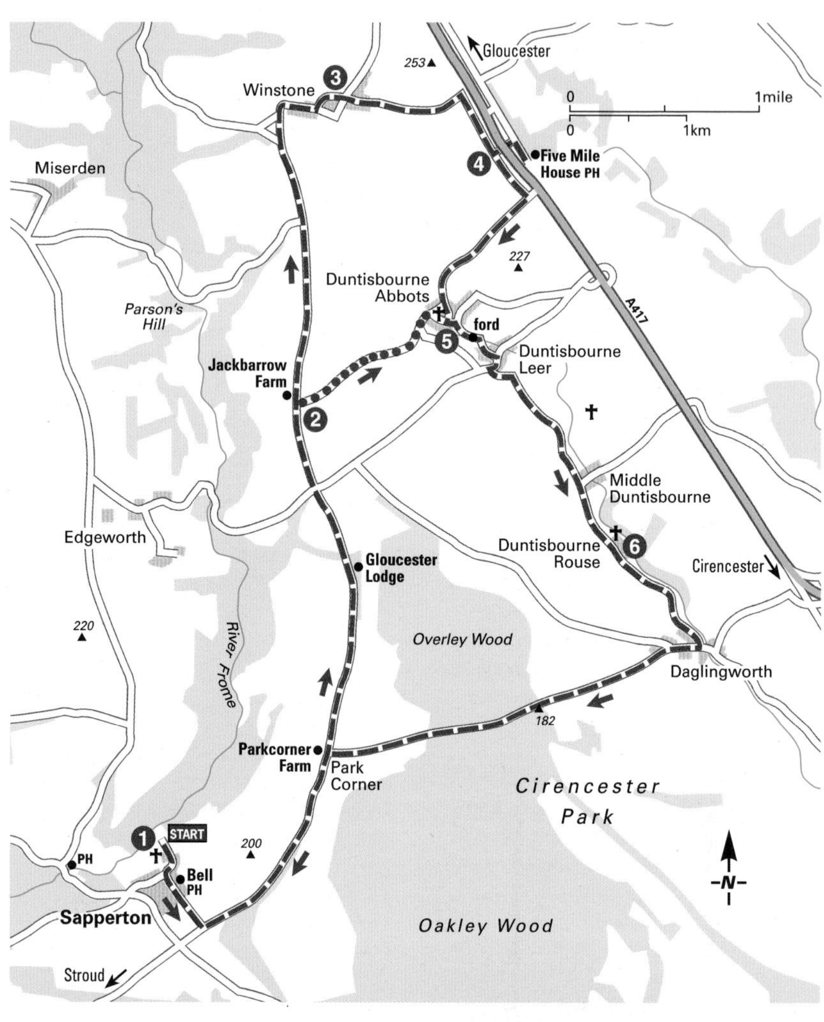

soon becomes wooded and before long reaches Middle Duntisbourne. Keep right on the main lane and, just over the crest of the hill, keep a look out for the lych-gate entrance to **Duntisbourne Rouse**'s church as it comes up on the left.

6 Carry on downhill, sticking with the main lane as it twists into Daglingworth. At a junction beside a telephone box, pedal right to **Park Corner** and **Sapperton**. Climb gently away, keeping left when the lane forks at the edge of the village. There follows an undemanding 0.75 mile (1.2km) climb onto the high ground, entering the **woodland** of the Earl of Bathurst's estate towards the top of the hill. Beyond, the road falls away gently to **Park Corner**, where you should turn left towards Sapperton. Follow your outward route back to the starting point, not forgetting that you must make a right turn in order to drop back past The Bell.

The Five Mile House

Despite undergoing some modernisation after remaining in a time warp for decades, this 300-year-old country tavern remains a classic, unspoiled gem and well worth lingering in over a pint or two of local Donnington BB. The tiny, bare-boarded bar and the simple tap room up the flagstoned hallway preserve an old-fashioned feel, the latter featuring two ancient high-backed settles, and a wood-burning stove in an old fireplace. Rightly, no food is served in these timeless rooms that are perfect for conversation and quaffing of ale. There is a smart dining room extension to the rear as well as a cellar bar and a family room. Escape to the lovely garden in summer and enjoy the country views.

about the pub

The Five Mile House
Lane's End
Duntisbourne Abbots
Cirencester, Gloucestershire GL7 7JR
Tel: 01285 821432

DIRECTIONS: off A417 north west of Cirencester, signposted Duntisbourne Abbots & Services, turn right, then right again and follow 'no through' road sign

PARKING: 30

OPEN: daily

FOOD: daily

BREWERY/COMPANY: free house

REAL ALE: Donnington BB, Timothy Taylor Landlord, Young's Bitter, guest beer

Food

The freshly prepared food includes lunchtime sandwiches, ham, egg and chips and deep-fried cod and chips. More imaginative evening dishes may feature pork glazed with honey and mustard and neck of lamb with rosemary jelly. Sunday roast lunches.

Family facilities

Well-behaved children are welcome in the family room. Smaller portions of some adult dishes can be prepared.

Alternative refreshment stops

Back in Sapperton, try The Bell at Sapperton.

☛ Where to go from here

Cirencester is not far away. As well as the Corinium Museum (www.cotswolds.gov.uk) and the largest parish church in England, you can explore Cirencester Park. This fine estate was partly designed by the poet Alexander Pope for Lord Bathurst and can be accessed from Sapperton.

Cotswold Water Park

Abandoned gravel pits create havens for wildlife and fabulous opportunities for watersports.

Water Park wildlife

Overlying the Oxford clay south of Cirencester is a shallow deposit of gravel, which has been exploited since the 1920s for use in building and construction. As individual workings have been abandoned, they have been flooded to create a landscape peppered with almost 100 lakes, causeways and small islands. Left to nature, many of the fringes have developed as marsh and wetland, and the area has become an important site for both resident and migratory water birds. Two of the hides are passed on the cycle ride, and amongst the birds over-wintering here you can expect to see green sandpiper, golden-eye, great northern diver and teal, and if you are lucky, you might even hear the booming of a bittern. In summer you will glimpse many familiar garden birds, also reed and sedge warblers and perhaps a nightingale. Attracted by the water are oystercatchers, shelduck and several species of grebe, and predatory birds such as merlin, harriers and even ospreys make an appearance. Flower-rich meadows attract a variety of butterflies, and dragonflies and damselflies are found around the shores.

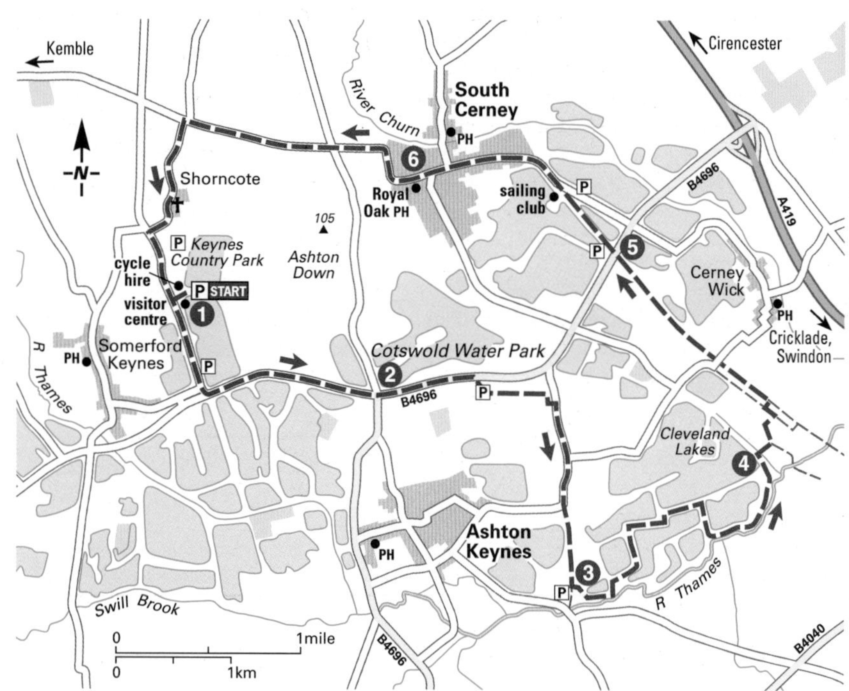

22

2h30 | 10.75 MILES | 17.3 KM | LEVEL 123

The railway track that takes the ride into South Cerney formed part of the Midland Junction line between Cheltenham and Southampton until its closure during the mid-1960s. Plans are underway to restore part of the line south of Cricklade. Look out for the unusual brick-arched bridges encountered along the way. Their intricate design suggests something more appropriate to the galleries beneath a Roman amphitheatre rather than mere props to carry a road.

the ride

1 Leaving the car park past the visitor centre, follow a shore path to a second smaller car park, there emerging onto **Spratsgate Lane**. Turn left, winding around left again at its end to join Spine Road (West) towards Ashton Keynes. After 1 mile (1.6km) at a crossroads, dismount and cross to continue along Spine Road (East), the busy **B4696** to Cirencester. A few yards/metres along, there is a dedicated cycle track beside it on the left, but be careful for it is bounded by drainage ditches and gutters, with gullies intruding into the pathway.

2 Follow that for another 0.5 mile (800m) to the **Clayhill car park** on the right, again dismounting to reach the entrance. At the back of the car park, a bridlepath leaves to the left, signed to **South Cerney**. Through a gap in the hedge, carry on ahead at the edge of a field, crossing an access road, which leads to a **working gravel pit** (watch out for moving wagons). At the far end, swing onto a track beside the workings. At another quarry road go forward to a break in the hedge opposite, cross a track and continue on the contained path between a lake and

MAP: OS Explorer 169 Cirencester & Swindon

START/FINISH: Keynes Country Park (pay and display car park); grid ref: SU026958

TRAILS/TRACKS: gravel cycle tracks

LANDSCAPE: low-lying countryside speckled with the lakes of abandoned gravel pits

PUBLIC TOILETS: at car park

TOURIST INFORMATION: Cirencester, tel 01285 654180

CYCLE HIRE: Go By Cycle, Lake 31, Keynes Country Park, Spratsgate Lane, Shorncote, tel: 07970 419208

THE PUB: Royal Oak, South Cerney

! Beware of sleeper barriers and take care on the minor roads and at three main road crossings. Tracks shared with pedestrians and horses and may be muddy after rain

Getting to the start

The Cotswold Water Park lies 4 miles (6.4km) south of Cirencester. From the A419, follow the B4696, continuing ahead at a crossroads north of Ashton Keynes along Spine Road (West). The main car park and visitor centre is then off right along Spratsgate Lane.

Why do this cycle ride?

Cotswold Water Park encompasses some 14,000 acres (5670ha). This route passes both working and abandoned gravel pits, which provide a haven for wildlife. Vast numbers of water birds can be seen. Areas are set aside for watersports and fishing.

Researched and written by: Dennis Kelsall

Fridays Ham Lane, signed 'Waterhay'. It later ends abruptly and you must cross the lane, but be careful, as you are on a blind bend. The ongoing path leads beside a second lake, shortly reaching a junction.

3 The way lies left, marked **'Thames Path'**, angularly twisting along old field margins that now separate a succession of lakes. The way passes a bird hide and then through gates demarking the **Manor Brook Lake** fishing area. Over a crossing track the route briefly joins the infant Thames and then passes a small car park. Carry on until you reach the gated pedestrian entrance to **Cleveland Lakes** (where there is another bird hide) and here, go right over a bridge spanning Shire Ditch.

4 Ride on beside a field to meet a broad track and go left towards **South Cerney**. Go left again at the next junction but after 250yds (229m) look for a broad unmarked track on the right. It connects with a parallel **disused railway track**, turn left along it. Tunnelled by trees, the track shortly passes beneath a viaduct carrying the road from Cerney Wick and continues for another 0.75 mile (1.2km) before reaching the B4696 at **Bridge car park**.

5 Cross the road with care. Opposite, the path passes under more arches and resumes its onward course to South Cerney, eventually ending beside the village **sailing club**. The road leads on into the village. Keep ahead at a junction by the old cross towards Ewen and Ashton Keynes, shortly passing the **Royal Oak**, a convenient spot to break the journey.

6 Stay with the road as it meanders past **playing fields** out of the village, before long reaching a crossroads with a busier road. Go forward, signed to Ewen and Kemble, for a little over 0.75 mile (1.2km) then turn off left onto a narrow and, in places, poorly surfaced lane to **Shorncote**. It winds past **Shorncote Manor Farm** and its attendant church, shortly emerging onto Spratsgate Lane. **The Keynes Country Park Visitor Centre** is then less than 0.5 mile (800m) to the left.

House and garden at South Cerney

Royal Oak

In 1997 human remains were found during excavations for an extension to this popular village local close to the Cotswold Water Park. Now thought to have been built on an early Saxon graveyard, the original old cottage first became a pub in 1850. Sympathetic additions over the years have created spacious bars and a dining area, while outside the large and pleasant rear garden features a big terrace and a summer marquee. Come for good-value home-cooked food and rotating real ales from Courage, Adnams, Fuller's and Wychwood breweries.

Food

Traditional pub food includes standard snacks (filled baps, sandwiches and egg and chips), home-made soups, salads, giant Yorkshire puddings with sausages and onion gravy, and lasagne and regular specials such as steak and kidney pie and Barnsley lamb chops.

Family facilities

Children are welcome in the pub where youngsters have their own menu to choose from. Plenty of space in the safe summer garden.

Alternative refreshment stops

Café at Country Park Visitor Centre; other pubs in South Cerney.

☛ Where to go from here

There's plenty to see and do at Keynes Water Park (www.waterpark.org). Further afield, you can take a ride on the Swindon and Cricklade Railway or visit the Bristol Aero Collection at Kemble (www.bristolaero.i12.com)

about the pub

Royal Oak
High Street, South Cerney
Cirencester, Gloucestershire GL7 5UP
Tel: 01285 860298

DIRECTIONS: village signposted off the A419, 3 miles (4.8km) south east of Cirencester; pub located on the left along the road towards Ewen

PARKING: 16

OPEN: daily; all day Friday, Saturday and Sunday

FOOD: daily; all day Friday, Saturday and Sunday

BREWERY/COMPANY: free house

REAL ALE: Courage Best, Marston's Pedigree, guest beers

23

Chedworth Roman Villa

Discover a Roman villa set in a picturesque fold of the Cotswold Hills.

Roman villa

Set amid idyllic Cotswold countryside, the Roman villa at Chedworth is perhaps the finest discovered in Britain. The area was well populated during the occupation, and Corinium (Cirencester) was the second largest Roman town in the country. The villa was discovered by chance in 1864 by a gamekeeper digging to retrieve a lost ferret. Subsequent excavation has revealed an extensive site containing some wonderfully preserved features. First built around AD 120, it was enlarged and added to over the next 300 years, and some 32 rooms have been identified, including kitchens, living and dining rooms, latrines and bath houses as well as outside courtyard and garden areas. Bathing was an important element in Roman life, a social occasion rather than simply a means of keeping clean. The baths here were obviously well used, judging by the wear on the floors, and in addition to cold plunges there were wet and dry hot baths. The hypocaust is clearly revealed, showing how hot air circulated beneath the floors and within the walls to provide all-round heating. But perhaps the most spectacular feature is the mosaic flooring. The one in the dining room

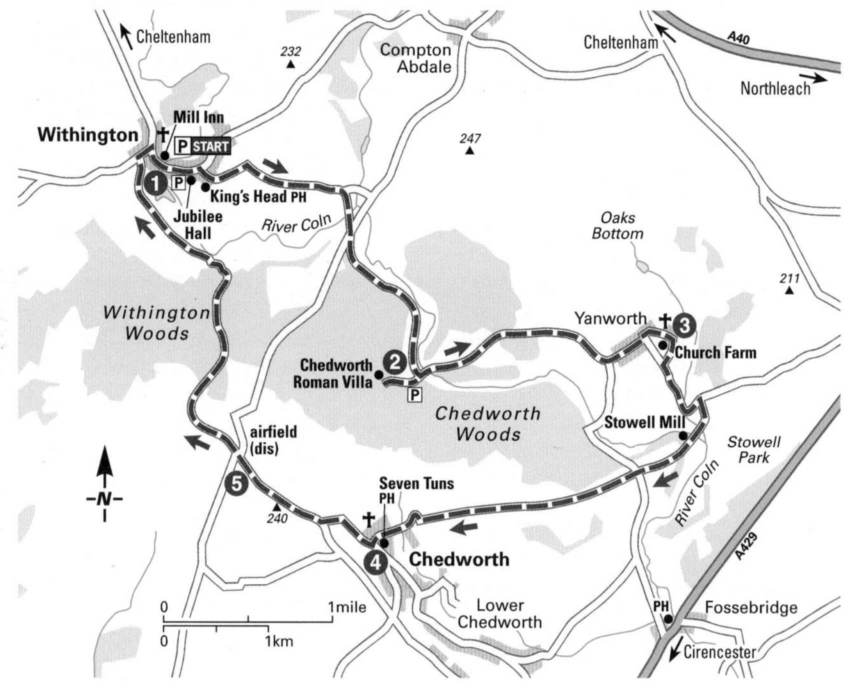

Above: Mosaic at Chedworth Roman Villa
Next page: Foundations of the Roman villa

is particularly brilliant, depicting young boys who represent the four seasons, although sadly, autumn is missing.

the ride

1 From **The Mill Inn** car park, go left between the abutments of a dismantled railway bridge to rise past the entrance to **Jubilee Hall**, which is on the right. At the next turning, go right, signed 'Yanworth' and 'Roman Villa'. After the **King's Head**, leave the village behind, the narrow lane climbing over a hill then falling in a long descent into the Coln valley. There is a fine view ahead across the wolds, although it may be marred for some by the lines of pylons to be seen marching over the hills. Cross the river at the bottom and climb to a crossroads. Ahead the lane undulates easily along the wooded edge, shortly reaching a junction where the **Roman villa** is signed off on the right.

3h00 — 10.75 MILES — 17.3 KM — LEVEL 123

MAP: OS Explorer OL45 The Cotswolds
START/FINISH: The Mill Inn, Withington (ask permission first); grid ref: SP032154
TRAILS/TRACKS: country lanes throughout
LANDSCAPE: steeply rolling hills cleaved by deep, wooded valleys
PUBLIC TOILETS: none on route
TOURIST INFORMATION: Cirencester, tel 01285 654180
CYCLE HIRE: none locally
THE PUB: The Mill Inn, Withington
! Several long, steep climbs; take care on country lanes

Getting to the start

Some 6 miles (9.7km) south east of Cheltenham, Withington lies in the valley of the River Coln and is most easily reached along a minor lane from the A436. If The Mill Inn is busy, use a car park by the Jubilee Hall on the other side of the old railway bridge.

Why do this cycle ride?

The Coln is one of the prettiest rivers in the Cotswolds and below Withington it winds through a lovely, deep wooded valley. The ride begins in Withington, climbing a shoulder to drop back into the Coln valley, where it passes a Roman villa. The climb to Yanworth is rewarded by medieval wall paintings in its church. On the other side of the valley, the route is via Chedworth before finally returning to Withington past a disused wartime airfield.

Researched and written by: Dennis Kelsall

2 Rejoin the lane at this point after visiting the villa and re-cross the river, the way signed to Yanworth and Northleach. After another stiff pull, the lane runs more easily over Yanworth Common, eventually reaching a junction. Keep ahead towards **Yanworth**. Pedal through the village, but at the far side where the road bends to Northleach, go left. The lane winds around and down to the church.

3 Carry on down the hill below **Church Farm**, swinging beneath paddocks to a junction. Go left and drop across the bottom of the valley, pulling away steeply beyond to a junction. Turn right towards **Chedworth**, descending back into the vale to re-cross the river by **Stowell Mill**. Another short climb follows, soon levelling to reach a crossroads. Keep ahead, still towards Chedworth, the way rising steadily away. Eventually the lane begins to fall, the gradient increasing as it twists through sharp bends into Chedworth. Over a stream at the bottom, it is up again, to the **Seven Tuns pub**, opposite which is the church.

4 Continue past the pub and take the lane ahead at the junction above, signed to Withington. At the top of the hill, go right, shortly passing the runways of a **disused airfield**.

5 Carry on at the crossing and then bear right to join a busier road, still following signs to **Withington**. Entering woodland there begins a long descent, which later steepens to a sharp right-hand bend. Emerging from the trees, the way undulates for another 0.75 mile (1.2km) into Withington. Keep cycling along the main lane as it winds through the village, turning right opposite the church for the return to The Mill Inn.

The Mill Inn

Splendid low-beamed ceilings, large open fireplaces, stone- and oak-panelled walls and worn flagstone floors combine with simple rustic furnishings and country style artefacts to re-create the original atmosphere of this 400-year-old former corn mill and local brewhouse. Right up until 1914 the landlord was listed as an innkeeper and keeper of the watermill. The pub stands in a deep valley on the banks of the River Coln, surrounded by beech and chestnut trees, and it has a lovely riverside garden, equipped with 50 tables and complete with friendly ducks, providing an idyllic post-ride setting for peaceful summer drinking. It is one of the few country pubs in the south where you can quaff Samuel Smith's beers.

about the pub

The Mill Inn
Withington, Cheltenham
Gloucestershire GL54 4BE
Tel: 01242 890204

DIRECTIONS: see Getting to the start
PARKING: 60
OPEN: daily
FOOD: daily
BREWERY/COMPANY: Samuel Smith Brewery
REAL ALE: Samuel Smith Best & Old Brewery Bitter
ROOMS: 3 en suite

Food

Menu choices include a selection of chargrills, fish specials and vegetarian options. Other dishes might include minty lamb casserole, creamy pork and mushroom pepperpot, steak and ale pie, home-baked crusty baguettes, ploughman's lunches, and a range of 'basket meals' – a food concept said to have originated here in the 1950s.

Family facilities

Families can expect a warm welcome and good provision for children. There's a family area in the pub, youngsters have their own menu and the toilets are equipped with baby-changing facilities. Children should be well supervised in the riverside garden.

Alternative refreshment stops

On the route you will pass the Seven Tuns in Chedworth village and the King's Head at Withington.

☛ Where to go from here

Explore Chedworth Roman Villa, one of the finest Romano-British villas in Britain, or head for Northleach to visit Keith Harding's World of Mechanical Music, a living museum of self-playing musical instruments (www.mechanicalmusic.co.uk).

The Upper Windrush Valley and the Slaughters

Explore the lush countryside around two of the Cotswolds' most famous villages.

The Slaughters

Bubbling from a spring in a secluded fold of the Cotswold hills, the River Eye embarks on a short but pretty journey past the Slaughters before becoming lost in the River Windrush, just a couple of miles further on below Bourton-on-the-Water. But for their unashamed loveliness, the two tiny villages would probably have escaped the notice of the modern world. Despite their popularity, they have remained unspoiled, resisting large car parks and commercial gift shops. At Lower Slaughter, you can visit a corn mill, which, although dating only from the 19th century, continues the tradition of a succession of earlier mills that have occupied the site since the Normans arrived on these shores. It houses a small shop, tea room, and museum which shows how grist milling has been carried out over the centuries.

Despite the close proximity of the two villages, Upper Slaughter has a completely different character to its neighbour. The cottages clustered around The Square were

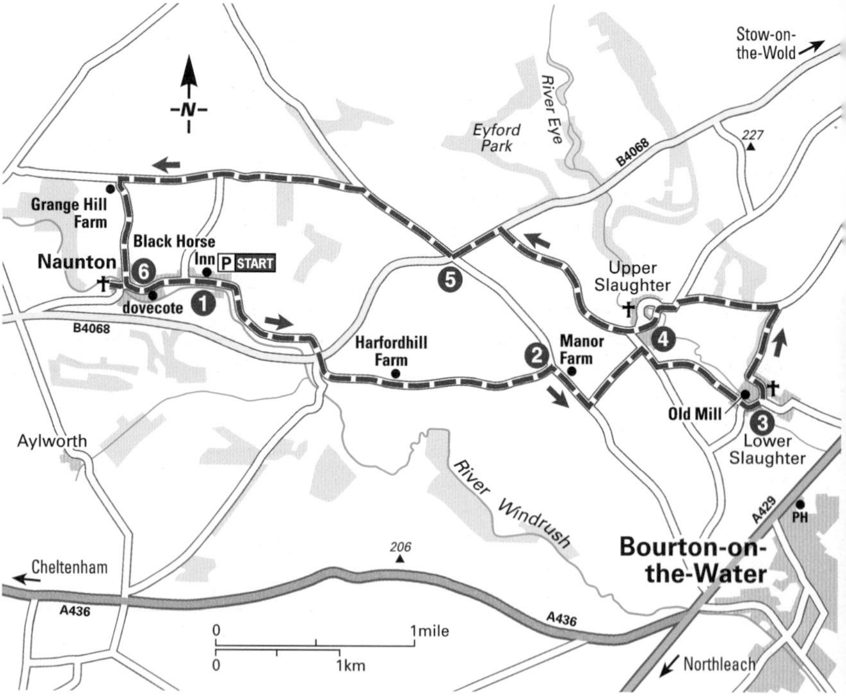

The River Eye passing through Upper Slaughter

3h00 | 9 MILES | 14.5 KM | LEVEL 123

reconstructed in 1906 by the great architect Sir Edward Lutyens, the designer of New Delhi, while a little earlier, the Victorian vicar of the Norman church, the Reverend Francis E Witts wrote *The Diary of a Cotswold Parson*.

Back in Naunton, the impressive dovecote is a rare survivor of its type, the roof sporting four gables and topped by a louvre to permit access by the birds. It is thought to date from around 1600 and was built to provide the lord of the manor with fresh meat during the winter months.

the ride

1 Starting with the pub on your left, follow the lane out of the village, as yet pedalling easily along the bottom of the **Windrush valley**. At a crossroads with the B4068, the honeymoon comes to an end as you take the leftmost of the two lanes opposite. Tunnelled in trees, it climbs steeply away, but before long you can start changing up through the gears as the gradient levels past **Harfordhill Farm**. Your exertion is rewarded by a fine view across the wolds as you continue to a junction.

2 Go right past **Manor Farm**, and then left at the next turning, signed to Upper and Lower Slaughter. Free-wheeling down, watch your speed, for there is a T-junction at the bottom where you should go right to **Lower Slaughter**. Keep with the main lane as it shortly bends left in front of a junction and sweeps around beside the River Eye into the centre of the village.

MAP: OS Explorer OL 45 The Cotswolds

START/FINISH: The Black Horse Inn, Naunton (ask permission first); grid ref: SP234119

TRAILS/TRACKS: country lanes

LANDSCAPE: rolling Cotswold countryside between the valleys of the Windrush and Eye

PUBLIC TOILETS: none on route

TOURIST INFORMATION: Stow-on-the-Wold, tel 01451 831082

CYCLE HIRE: none locally

THE PUB: The Black Horse Inn, Naunton

! Several stiff and one steep ascent, and a long downhill stretch. Suitable for fitter, older family groups

Getting to the start

Naunton is located just off the B4068, 4.5 miles (7.2km) west of Stow-on-the-Wold. Leaving the main road, follow a narrow lane through the village to find The Black Horse Inn, from which the ride begins.

Why do this cycle ride?

The twin villages of the Slaughters are the epitome of the Cotswold village, and although both can become unbearably crowded on a fine weekend during the summer, they display nothing but charm on a quieter day. Inevitably, the ride encounters a succession of hills, but take your time, and you will discover scenic beauty in this pastoral countryside that is often missed when travelling by car.

Researched and written by: Dennis Kelsall

3 At a junction in front of **St Mary's Church**, go left, passing through the more recent part of the village and the cricket green before climbing steadily away. After 0.33 mile (500m) at a bend, turn sharp left to **Upper Slaughter**, pedalling over a gentle rise before dropping to a junction. To the left the lane falls more steeply, winding sharply to a bridge at the bottom of the hill. Climb away on the far side to a small raised green at the heart of the village, above which to the right stands the **church**. Don't leave without having a look at the **ford**, which lies over the hill behind the church. The high ground opposite was the site of an early Norman stronghold.

4 The route continues with the main lane through the village to a junction. Go right towards Cheltenham. There follows a prolonged pull out of the valley, which eventually eases to a junction with the **B4068**. To the left the climb resumes for another 0.25 mile (400m) to a crossroads.

5 Turn right on a lane, signed to **Cotswold Farm Park**, enjoying a much easier 0.5 mile (800m). At a fork, bear left to Guiting Power and Winchcombe, the gently undulating road offering more expansive views to the south. Go past the first turning off left, signed to Naunton, continuing for a further 0.5 mile (800m) to a second turning, also on the left by **Grange Hill Farm**. An unmarked narrow lane, it drops steeply into the valley. Go carefully as it winds sharply to a junction at the edge of Naunton.

6 The way back to The Black Horse Inn is to the left, but first have a look at the **church**, which lies a short distance along to the right. As you return to the pub, another deviation is merited, this time, turning right just after the **Baptist church** to see Naunton's historic **dovecote**.

A cyclist passes through Lower Slaughter village without encountering other traffic

The Black Horse Inn

The setting is a typical Cotswold village sunk deep in the beautiful Windrush Valley, much beloved of locals, ramblers and cyclists alike. Original flagstones, blackened beams, open log fires, simple tables and chairs and fine oak pews exude simple rural charm in the main bar while the lounge offers a smaller, snugger retreat. Built of honey-coloured stone and dating from the 1870s, the pub is renowned for its home-cooked food, Donnington real ales and utterly peaceful bed and breakfast.

about the pub

The Black Horse Inn
Naunton, Stow-on-the-Wold
Gloucestershire GL54 3AD
Tel: 01451 850565
www.blackhorsenaunton.com

DIRECTIONS: see Getting to the Start
PARKING: 12
OPEN: daily; all day Saturday & Sunday
FOOD: not Sunday or Monday evenings
BREWERY/COMPANY: Donnington Brewery
REAL ALE: Donnington BB & SBA
ROOMS: 1 en suite

Food

Dishes range from ploughman's lunch, filled baguettes and jacket potatoes to some accomplished main dishes: steak and kidney pudding, grilled trout, chicken breast with Stilton and bacon, salmon fillet in saffron sauce, and local game in season. There's also the day's selection of 'sinful sweets'!

Family facilities

Families are welcome inside the pub. Smaller portions of adult meals and high chairs are available.

Alternative refreshment stops

Hotels for lunches and cream teas in both the Slaughters; café at The Mill in Lower Slaughter.

☛ Where to go from here

Spend some time in Bourton-on-the-Water. Children will enjoy the fabulous toy collection and the cars at the Cotswold Motoring Museum and Toy Collection (www.cotswold-motor-museum.com), the perfect replica of a Cotswold village at the Model Village, and a visit to Birdland Park and Gardens, a natural setting of woodland, river and gardens inhabited by more than 500 birds.

Burford and the Windrush Valley

Discover ancient village churches, built by master craftsmen from local stone that was later used to repair Westminster Abbey.

Windrush Valley churches

The wealth generated by medieval sheep farming is evident in Burford's church, a magnificent edifice topped by a soaring spire, which is said to be one of the highest in Oxfordshire. Yet although the surrounding churches may be more modest in scale, they each have qualities worthy of investigation. At Little Barrington there is magnificent Norman stonework around the doorway, whilst Great Barrington's church contains an Elizabethan effigy of a Captain Bray, unusually depicting the sword on the right. Pardoned by his queen for killing a man in anger, Bray swore never again to draw his sword with his right hand. The church at Taynton has fine carving decorating the door and windows, with corbels fashioned into heads overlooking the nave. The font, too, is remarkable, adorned with angels, evangelists and other figures, including a mermaid.

At Swinbrook you will find two splendid Tudor-style monuments and the graves of Nancy, Unity and Pamela Mitford, whose family held Asthall Manor. Nancy is known for her novels, which included *Love in a Cold Climate* and Unity gained notoriety because of her association with leading Nazis. At St Nicholas's, Asthall, you can see one of the few surviving 'blacksmith' clocks. Widford's church is reached by a footpath off on the right after crossing the river by Widford Mill. Isolated after the village was abandoned to escape the plague, its walls have sombre 14th-century frescoes, grimly reminding man of his mortality. The building occupies the site of a Roman villa, but a famous tessellated floor, discovered beneath the chancel, is sadly now covered to prevent vandalism.

the ride

1 Riding out of the car park, turn left up Guildenford and then, opposite the **Royal Oak**, go right along Witney Street. At the busy crossroads in the centre of town, cross diagonally into Sheep Street and head past the **hospital** out of the village. After 0.5 mile (800m), just as the road begins to climb, look for a very narrow, unsigned lane leaving on the right. It gently rises and falls along the side of the Windrush Valley, offering picturesque views over the low-lying meadows bordering the river. Although poorly surfaced initially, the lane improves towards **Little Barrington**, passing the village's tiny church along the way.

2 At the end of the lane, drop right beside the green, shortly going right again over the river towards Great Barrington. Beyond **The Fox Inn**, a second bridge heralds a short but steepish pull into Great Barrington, passing the entrances to **Barrington Park** and the nearby church at the top on your left. Carry on into the village and keep right in front of the **war memorial** for Taynton, the way tracing long undulations along the valley side. The area is famed for its fine stone and the masons who worked it. **Taynton** provided stone for the repair of Westminster Abbey and the Strong family

The Fettiplace Monument in Swinbrook's church

25

3h00 | 13.5 MILES | 21.7 KM | LEVEL 123

MAP: OS Explorer OL45 The Cotswolds
START/FINISH: car park in Burford; grid ref: SP253122
TRAILS/TRACKS: unclassified country roads and lanes, two short sections on main roads
LANDSCAPE: rolling countryside bordering the River Windrush
PUBLIC TOILETS: at car park
TOURIST INFORMATION: Burford, tel 01993 823558
CYCLE HIRE: none locally
THE PUB: The Fox Inn, Great Barrington
! Care to be taken crossing main road in Burford and on two stretches of main road later in ride. The ride is undulating

Getting to the start

Burford stands by a crossroads of the A40 between Oxford – 23 miles (37km) and Cheltenham – 20 miles (32.2km) and the A361 north from Swindon. A car park, from which the ride begins, is signed along Church Lane from the A361 in the town centre.

Why do this cycle ride?

The ancient wool town of Burford is an attractive focal point for this exploration of the secluded Windrush Valley, presented here as an 'unclosed' figure-of-eight circuit that allows two shorter rides. Surrounded by the rolling Cotswold hills, the Valley is lined with pretty small villages.

Researched and written by: Dennis Kelsall

from Barrington served as master masons for the building of Sir Christopher Wren's St Paul's Cathedral.

3 At Taynton, the **church** is set back from the lane on the right. It was once part of a small monastery belonging to the French abbey of St Denis, which was dissolved by Edward IV and given to the Abbot of Tewkesbury. Cycle through the hamlet and keep ahead towards Burford, eventually reaching a junction with the A424.

4 At this point you can shorten the ride by going forward and then right at a mini roundabout to return to Burford. Otherwise head left up the hill for 200yds (183m) before turning right on a narrow lane. It winds past **Manor Farm** over Westhall Hill, then falls beyond to join the A361. Follow it left through **Fulbrook**, very soon leaving at the second of two turnings on the right, a single track lane signed to Swinbrook. It climbs steadily away between fields and past woodland, later dipping to cross the head of **Dean Bottom** before descending to a junction. **Swinbrook** lies to the right, where another church on the right, St Mary's, merits a visit.

5 Carry on beyond the church for another 200yds (183m) before turning left uphill to leave the village. Keep right with the main lane, still gaining height along the valley side. Later levelling to a junction, go right to **Asthall**, dropping to cross the base of the flat valley where a sporadic line of pollarded willows marks the course of the river. Follow

the lane around right into the village, winding left in front of the church before turning right by the entrance of the **manor**.

6 Head away along the lane to a crossroads, where to the right, just across the river, you will find a welcoming pub, **The Swan Inn**. The onward way, however, lies straight over, along the pretty valley, through the tiny hamlet of **Widford** and eventually back to Burford.

Great Barrington

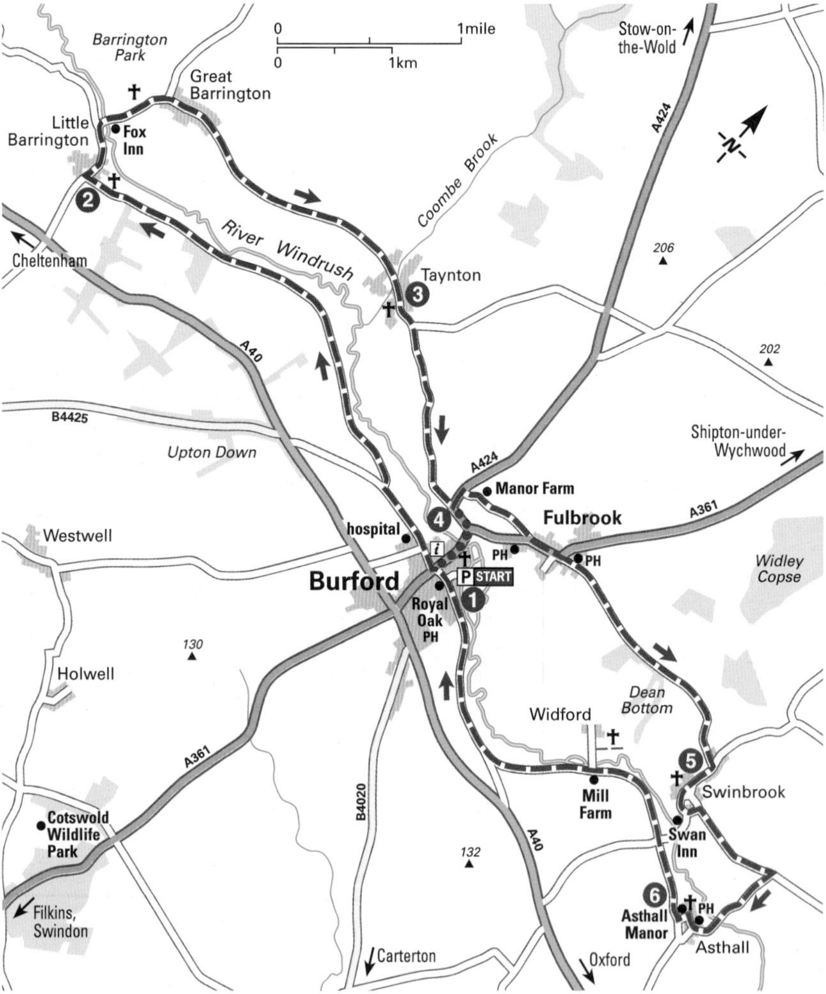

The Fox Inn

about the pub

The Fox Inn
Great Barrington, Burford
Gloucestershire OX18 4TB
Tel: 01451 844385
www.foxinnbarrington.co.uk

DIRECTIONS: The village is signposted off the A40 3 miles (4.8km) west of Burford and the pub is located beside the River Windrush
PARKING: 60
OPEN: daily; all day
FOOD: daily
BREWERY/COMPANY: Donnington Brewery
REAL ALE: Donnington BB & SBA
ROOMS: 4 en suite

A genuinely unspoiled little Cotswold pub, built in the 17th century with the local honey-coloured stone and picturesquely set beside the gently meandering River Windrush. Its charm is of the simple alehouse sort, with low ceilings, stone walls, rustic furnishings, blazing winter log fires, and time-honoured pub games in the small main bar. Modern-day trends do exist here – the former skittle alley now houses a restaurant with river views and a splendid wall mural of the pretty valley, and four comfortable en suite rooms. Lovely river and lakeside gardens and a heated rear terrace make The Fox a great summer pub, in fact the best summer watering-hole for miles. Added attractions include the excellent local Donnington beer, heady farm ciders, and good, home-made food.

Food
Separate lunch and dinner menus offer a varied choice of meals. At lunchtime, apart from sandwiches and traditional dishes such as battered cod and chips, home-cooked ham, egg and chips, and beef and ale pie, blackboards may list Thai-style tuna, spinach, leek and chestnut pie, salmon fishcakes, and seasonal game, perhaps pigeon breast casseroled with mushrooms and red wine.

Family facilities
A genuine warm welcome awaits children who will enjoy the splendid lake and riverside gardens (care and supervision required). Inside, there are high chairs and smaller portions of adult dishes are served.

Alternative refreshment stops
You are spoilt for choice in Burford. Take your pick from hotel restaurants, pubs and tea rooms. Along the route there's the Carpenter's Arms and Mason's Arms in Fulbrook, The Swan at Swinbrook and the Maytime Inn at Asthall.

☛ Where to go from here
The Cotswold Wildlife Park and Gardens (www.cotswoldwildlifepark.co.uk) is a great venue for gardeners and their children, with rare and endangered species in parkland and gardens, and there's a narrow gauge railway and an adventure playground. Learn more about the skills of spinning and weaving woollen fabric at the Cotswold Woollen Weavers in Filkins.

Acknowledgements

The Automobile Association would like to thank the following photographers, companies and picture libraries for their assistance in the preparation of this book.

Abbreviations for the picture credits are as follows: - (t) top; (b) bottom; (l) left; (r) right; (AA) AA World Travel Library.

Front cover AA/J Sparks; Back cover AA/N Hicks; 3 AA/J Sparks; 6/7 AA N Ray; 12/13 AA/C Jones; 13t AA/R Tenison; 15 AA/S Viccars; 16/17 AA/S Viccars; 19 AA/S Viccars; 20 AA/S Viccars; 21 AA/C Jones; 23 AA/S Viccars; 24/25 AA/S Viccars; 27 AA/S Viccars; 28 AA/S Viccars; 29 AA/C Jones; 31 AA/S Viccars; 32 AA/S Viccars; 35 AA/S Viccars; 37 AA/S Viccars; 39 Christie Estates; 40 AA/R Moss; 41 AA/S Viccars; 43 AA/S Viccars; 44/45 AA/J O'Carroll; 47 AA/S Viccars; 48 AA/S Viccars; 49 AA/S Viccars; 51 AA/S Viccars; 53 AA/S Viccars; 55 AA/S Viccars; 56 AA/ S Viccars; 57 AA/S Viccars; 59 AA/S Viccars; 60 AA/W Voysey; 61 AA/S Viccars; 63 AA/S Viccars; 64/65 AA/R Hall; 65t AA/R Moss; 67 AA/S Viccars; 68 AA/S Viccars; 71 AA/S Viccars; 72 AA/D Kelsall; 73 AA/ S & O Mathews; 75t AA/D Ireland; 75b AA/D Kelsall; 78 AA/R Ireland; 79 AA/ R Ireland; 81 AA/ D Kelsall; 82 AA/ D Kelsall; 83 AA/D Kelsall; 84 AA/ D Kelsall; 86 AA/ S & O Mathews; 87 AA/ D Kelsall; 88 AA/ D Ireland; 91 AA/ D Ireland; 92 AA/A Baker; 95 AA/D Kelsall; 97 AA/S Day; 98 AA/K Doran; 99 AA/D Kelsall; 101 AA/ R Surman; 102 AA/ R Surman; 103 AA/D Kelsall; 105 AA/S Day; 106 AA/S Day; 107 AA/D Kelsall; 109 AA/S Day; 110 AA/S Day; 111 AA/D Kelsall

Every effort has been made to trace the copyright holders, and we apologise in advance for any accidental errors. We would be happy to apply the corrections in the following edition of this publication.